SOMEONE SPECIAL

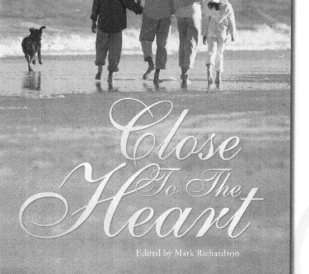

Close
To The
Heart

Edited by Mark Richardson

 Young**Writers**

First published in Great Britain in 2008 by
Young Writers, Remus House, Coltsfoot Drive,
Peterborough, PE2 9JX
Tel (01733) 890066   Fax (01733) 313524
Website: www.youngwriters.co.uk
All Rights Reserved

© Copyright Contributors 2008
SB ISBN 978-1-84431-585-7

Foreword

Our 'Someone Special' poetry competition
inspired aspiring young poets to show their admiration
for someone who has made an impact in their life.
What better way to let those closest know how
much they are appreciated.

Therefore we are delighted to present
'Someone Special – Close To The Heart'. After reading
through hundreds of entries it is clear the amount of
enthusiasm and love that went into writing these
poems, we're sure you'll agree they are an inspiring
and heart-warming read.

Young Writers was established in 1991 to
promote poetry and creative writing to school
children and encourage them to read, write and enjoy it.
Here at Young Writers we are sure you'll agree that this
special edition achieves our aim and celebrates today's
wealth of young writing talent. We hope you
enjoy *'Someone Special – Close To The Heart'*
for many years to come.

Mark Richardson, Editor

Contents

St Joan of Arc Catholic School, Rickmansworth

Stonehouse Primary School, Stonehouse

The Poems

For Flossie

I once read a motto,
'A boy needs two things in life: a dog
And a mother who lets him keep one,' it said.

But no one is complete without the love of a dog,
It's not only boys who need the wonderful joy
Of furry, unconditional, canine love.

A dog understands you in a special way
Picking up your feelings with a mystery sixth sense
Wet-nosed trust and wagging tail loyalty.

My dog is no different
She is getting old now and she wiffles in her sleep
But in the morning when I get up
And in the afternoon when I come home from school
She is there, waiting for me.

It is the best of feelings
Like seeing your best friend again
When you have been apart for too long and you can't stop smiling.

My dog cares about me
She thinks I am brilliant, no matter what happens
Or how much I doubt myself.

She trusts me to care for her
And she cares for me in return
That is why she is the most special person anyone could wish for!

Lissie Davidson (13)

A Poem For My Family

To my family, I love you,
Do you love me? I hope you do,
If you love me, say it out loud,
'Cause if you love me, I'll be proud.

To my family, I love Dad,
If he doesn't love me, I'll be sad,
To my family, I love Mum,
If she doesn't love me, I'll be glum.

To my family, I love Rhys,
If he loves me, I'll be pleased,
To my family, I love you all,
If you didn't love me, my life would fall.

Tomasin Roberts (9)

My Sister

I   gla is my sister
G lad she's not a mister
L ovely blonde hair
A lways there to care

S pecial to me
P eople have to agree
E ye colour, blue
C an you imagine it too
I   ntelligence is her thing
A lways happy to sing
L ike a lovely flower

That's why I love her!

Gledisa Musollari (10)

11

My Sister And I

She is funny
My sister is as the sun
She tells me funny things
My sister loves calling me Hannah Banana.

I kiss her as much as the sun kisses me
We love each other as much as God loves me and her
She loves me the most out of our family
I will never love anyone as much as my little sister.

Sometimes she is annoying
But she is little and I forgive her.
Hannah Richardson (12)

Untitled

I wish my grandma were alive
Instead of being in the clouds,
When we played together every day
We would sing songs out loud,
She made cakes with me
And took me to the park
And put me to bed
When it was dark,
We used to have so much fun
It was like having another Mum!
Stephanie Black (7)

What Do You Need In Life?

Ask yourself this, what do you need in life?
I say a friend,
A friend who is always there for you,
A friend who knows you,
I have that friend.

I have not known her long,
But I feel we have been friends all our lives,
When I see her in the morning,
She brings a smile to my face,
When she leaves in the evening,
She brings a tear to my eye.

All through the day she is there for me,
She comforts me in my sorrows
And shares in my joy,
When she's not there, I miss her
And think of her.

She's the best friend I could wish for
And I hope our friendship will never end,
There are so many spectacular things
I can say about her.

Her wonderful laugh never fails to bring a grin to my face,
Her eyes are always bright and shining,
Cold as ice is winter's touch, but she is like a summer day,
Warm and bright and always smiling,
A friend who is always there for me,
A friend who knows me,
I have that friend.

Ellen Feuchtwanger (13)

My Cat, Monty

He's cute an' fluffy,
A cuddly ball,
We miss him lots,
He was loved by all,
There wasn't a day with him not there,
He was always right next to me,
Long evening went by when we'd just sit
And watch something on TV,
He'd jump, he'd run, he'd hide and pounce
And follow me round and round the house,
But then the news
And my heart skipped a beat,
Nine lives of fun,
But then, defeat,
'Come back to me, don't go, come back!'
You just can't fill a gap as big as that,
So, five years on,
The hole is still there,
In the centre of my heart,
Dear friends, beware,
When something is missing,
Life's never the same,
Never underestimate,
You'll soon feel the pain,
He was my soulmate,
My fun and laughter,
I thought life was always,
'Happily ever after!'

Jenni Clark (12)

My Mother

Shahida lives by her name,
Cool, calm, collected, warm and sincere,
A great thinker who has millions of friends,
When I see her face, I see a big smile and laughter,
However, through that I see much pain that nobody sees.

I feel her pain through her touch,
My mother, my best friend, a fighter, a survivor and my life,
When I need her she is always there,
Her greatest gift is her beauty,
Her youthful looks, her ginormous personality,
But her greatest gift of all, is her kind, big heart.

In addition to that, there is her true gift,
To never hurt anyone because she loves everyone,
People that have been good to her
And people that have been bad
And all the people who have forgotten all the favours she did.

I admire my mother,
For being the hardest working mother,
This talent is truly gifted to my mother,
I solely devote this to you -
Love you, Mother Shahida.

Adam Mamaniat (13)

Gran, You're Special

My special person is my gran,
She is my biggest fan,
When I fall,
She will call,
'Are you alright?'

Sometimes at night,
She'll cuddle me tight
And whisper, 'I love you.'

When I cry,
She will sigh,
'Please don't be sad,
I am here to make you glad.'

Every night I say my prayers
And ask God to listen
And keep my gran safe and well,
As I have something I must tell.

I love my gran and my mother,
As I know, I have no other,
My gran likes her tea
And so do we,
But she takes no sugar,
As she is sweet for me.

Grant Burnett (8)

My Auntie, Gigi

You're my 'special someone',
You've been there since I was young.
For a baby, your name was hard to say,
So 'Auntie Lisa' was said in my own special way . . .
I could only call you 'Gigi',
This poem shows how much you mean to me.
You're always there for me when I am sad,
But you're a bit freaky and very mad!
I love you so, so, so very much,
I've probably got the best of luck!
I'm so glad you're my auntie, Gigi,
You mean the world to me!

Lola Scriven (9)

My Mum

I love my mum
Because she is really, really fun
I play with her all along
When I am dizzy
She's really quite busy
But I don't really care
Because I still love her all the time.

Niamh Paterson (7)

Cool Brother

Brother, you are so great
And you have lots of fate,
You are the best brother
And you are like no other!

Brother, you are the best,
No need to do my fabulous test,
You're just like me, intelligent and cool,
Hey, bro! You rule!

Osragli Elezi (9)

My Mum

My mum helps me
She sometimes takes us to the sea
My mum cares for me
She loves me lots and lots, you see
My mum takes us on holiday
She takes us out to play
My mum has blonde hair
When she was little, she had a teddy bear
Now you know a bit about my mum
She is the best mum under the sun!

Sam Underhill (9)

The Person Whom I Love

I love someone special,
She's always there for me,
She comforts me when I'm sad
And is always there to encourage me,
This special person is actually my mum,
She's always there, day and night for me.

Even if I'm not with her, she's still with me,
She's with me in my heart,
The most important place of all,
She spends part of her life only looking after me,
In my opinion, she's the best Mum you could ever have!

Tara McLeman (10)

My Mum Is My Best Friend

My mum is the one who stays in my heart
Every single day of my life
She is a very kind Mum who helps me
When things fall apart
The best thing about my mum, is that she buys nice stuff
For birthdays, Christmas and other times
She gives me a lot of things to make my life happy and enjoyable
I don't know where I would be without my mum
She's not just my mum, she is my best friend too!
I love my mum x!

Hayden Stevens (11)

My Best Friend!

She's smart and cute
Trust me, she's never mute
Not fussy like me
Sometimes a pussy she'll be
She's my best friend out of a dozen
And don't forget, she's also my cousin
She's a brunette queen
In her time, you'll never guess where she's been
Not rich, not poor
But middle class that's for sure
She's one in a million!

Kayleigh Thomas (11)

My Grandad

I love my grandad dearly
And even though he's gone
I feel like he's still with me.

I know he'll be remembered
Because he had so many friends
There are 80 round that corner
And 100 round that bend.

So, though my grandad's gone now
I know he's still beside me
Though I don't' know what he's doing now
He's there to love me and to guide me.

Rachel Watson (10)

My Great Aunt McFlurry

(IN MEMORY OF FLORRIE ALLSOP)

My great aunt McFlurry
Is always in a scurry
I often wonder where she goes
Hurrying off on her dainty little toes
She must be the most popular pensioner on the block
The leader of the flock
She has the funniest giggle
That makes her chin wiggle
I'm a bit concerned about my great aunt McFlurry
She's always been a bit of a worry
You'll never guess what happened the other day?
You won't believe it if I say
It's worse than the time she played the cymbals
I caught her watching The Fimbles
I do love my great aunt McFlurry
Even if she is a bit of a worry.

Grace Copperwhite (14)

Cherished Love

If I could have a wish come true
I would reverse time
And bring you back home to our family
And make everything fine.

You were taken from us from such an early start
And this has caused so much pain in our hearts.

You were so beautiful, playful and fun
Bringing joy and laughter to everyone.

We will cherish our love and memories of you
And pass it on to our children and grandchildren too.

When I look up at the sky at night
I feel comfort to know you are safe
In the arms of Jesus and the stars
That shine so bright.

Levi Tate (12)

My Sister

I love my sister
Because she's a pain in the bum
She puts me on the naughty stair
When I shouldn't be there
But Mum is fun!

Olivia Hoon (8)

Someone Special

Someone special to me
Is my special family, but
Someone sticks out in my mind
And he is very kind.

Granda Tom
Is what he's called
He is more special
Than them all.

Once I sat
On his knee
The tin whistle
He played for me.

He tells me stories
Of them all
He teaches me right
From wrong.

So when he reads
This from me
He knows how special
He means to me!

Stephanie Campbell (9)

Someone Special

Someone special, who could that be?
My pet I guess, no, not sure, you see.
That would be strange,
So my thoughts I have to arrange.

Who should I adore?
My mother all the more,
There are so many to choose,
But no match, the others I prefer to lose.

Reasons, so many, without a mask,
So this is an easy job and not a hard task.
She is beautiful, loving and caring,
Sweet, yet firm, always sharing.

Be good, she often said before bed,
Humbleness and meekness will take you far ahead.
You never seem to care or listen,
Now go brush your teeth and make them glisten.

My mum has got to be that special person I know,
'Cause I've lived with her a long time ago.
She is my best friend, I'm sure,
All those cuts and bruises, ready to cure.

Yes, I'm pleased to tell you who my idol be,
I've listed the main reasons, but above all, for me.
She is the person I love and cherish
And her words of encouragement will never perish.

Daneille Murdock (11)

Someone Special

My nana is someone special
My grandad is too
Nana knits jumpers for us
But that's something Grandad does not do,
We eat Nana's scrummy cobbler stew
We enjoy it, Grandad does too
They live by the seaside and each time we go
It's fun!
Did you know it rains everywhere
But Filey always gets the sun!
Nana and Grandad order it just for us
So we can play and build sandcastles all day
We live in Bolton, so when we go
We travel quite a long way
It's worth it though, cos when we go
Nana spoils us with her cooking
And Grandad gives me ginger nuts and chocolate
When no one is looking!
Nana had a birthday, she's 80 now
Grandad's not quite that old
They lived in the olden days
And things have changed, so I've been told
'Things aren't what they used to be'
Nana and Grandad keep telling me
But that's what makes them special
Their memories of yesterday
And the wonderful memories they make for me today.

Hannah Kilpatrick (9)

Untitled

My dad is happy and very funny
Gives me love, that's more than money
He shares my joy, gives me cuddles when I am sad
No one's better than my dad.

I love my dad, he is always there
Giving me his every care
Little things he does for me
My love for him is for all to see.

His arms around me, keeping me warm
Shuts the rain out and the storm
When I'm with him, I don't fear
He is always there to wipe a tear.

I always do as I am told
My dad says I'm better than gold
Helps me with homework and other stuff
My dad is big, strong and really tough.

Always picks me up from school
I think my dad is super cool
The very best friend I've ever had
No one in the world do I love, as much as my dad!

I do love my mummy too!

Laura Moran (9)

My Great Grandad

My special person is my great grandad
He is warm, with feelings
Full of love,
Special inside
And precious in my heart.

My great grandad is full with laughter,
Help for people,
Santa for some
And support for others.

Great grandad is no longer with us,
But I know he is looking down on me from high above.

Rosie Mason (10)

My Girlfriend, Kirsty

Kirsty, the girl of my dreams
I love you with all my heart
You give me support
When I get in difficult situations
You comfort me when I'm down

I love the colour of your hair
Your blue eyes always sparkle
You help me calm down when I am angry
We help each other in class
But most of all, I love your cuddles

Callum and Kirsty forever x!

Callum Stevens (12)

Half Term

Half term contains a lot of stresses
Fighting, shouting, begging, messes
We also have amazing fun
Which makes a change from boring school runs!

I know you may not think we're perfect
But we three boys, I swear, are worth it
Without you, Mum, our hearts are sunk
Even when you end up drunk!

You don't deserve our English weather
Florida, Spain, would be all the better
Because you're cool and deal with us
And rarely do you make a fuss!

You know us kids, not bad to the bone
We drive you to drink when we're at home
It won't be long, we'll fly the nest
And at last, you'll get that well-earned rest,
But Mum, half term is what we all love best!

Henry James Crisp (12)

Most Special Person

He always plays with me
And pays my football club fee,
He is a very funny and a hilarious man
A very keen football and tennis fan.

Every day his hair gets greyer
I would elect him as the mayor,
He is sporty and very fun
I reckon he could win an Olympic run.

He inspires me because he's simply great
When he confirms a time with me, he's never late,
I think he's a brilliant man
He takes after his mum, my gran.

He plays a part
In the middle of my heart,
When I'm feeling down or sad
From out of nowhere, there is my *dad!*

Jagjeevan Singh Sohal (11)

My Special Sister, Abbie

My sister, Abbie, you're my best friend,
Ballet dancer, princess, so let's pretend!
Rosy-red cheeks, dancing feet,
Always asking for more sweets!
Bubbly bright, cuddles delight,
Especially when we say goodnight!
Her favourite fairy is Tink,
Your favourite colour is definitely pink!
You're as sweet as lemonade,
Especially when we get up and raid!
When you're around, everything is sound,
Let's cherish the love we have found,
You're so cute, even when you tried playing my flute!
If Abbie's around, you feel great,
Sometimes she even makes me late!
However, Abbie, you're my sister and you're the best!
I could not love you any more!

Chloe Rushbrooke (10)

Someone Special

My brother tells me about what's right and what's wrong
I wish I were like him.

My mum teaches me how to save people's lives
I wish I were like her.

My dad inspires me to help others
I wish I were like him.

My granny teaches me about religion
I wish I were like her.

My instructor encourages me to challenge myself
I wish I were like him.

My teacher tells me to be content and happy
I'll just be myself.

Connor MacNeil (11)
Balmoral Primary School, Galashiels

My Mum

My mum, she's always there
And helps me in every possible way.

My mum, she's always loving me
And doing what's best for me.

My mum gives me my freedom
And allows me to go places.

My mum, she's always caring for me
And wanting what is best for me.

That's why she's the world's best Mum
And holds a special place in my heart.

Liam Rutherford (11)
Balmoral Primary School, Galashiels

My Mum

My mum never gives up on me
My mum always puts me right
My mum plays games with me
My mum does the housework
My mum is my nurse
My mum is the gardener
My mum works in a school
My mum is the dog walker
My mum is everything
My mum is special.

Ryan Shaw (11)
Balmoral Primary School, Galashiels

My Lamb

I want to be like her
Small and woolly.

I want to be like her
Funny and hilarious.

I want to be like her
Warm and cuddly.

I want to be like her
Always loving her food.

I want to be like her
Making someone feel special.

I want to be like her
Always wanting love.

I want to be like her
Never unhappy or sad.

Who do I want to be like?
My lamb, Softy.

Lucie Shand (11)
Balmoral Primary School, Galashiels

My Parents

If only I could be like my mum
She helps me with my homework.

If only I could be like my parents
Strong and healthy.

If only I could swim like my dad
It would be great.

If only I could cook like my mum
She is the best.

If only I could defeat my dad at football
I would be proud.

If only I knew I would grow up like them
My parents.

Kyle Dytor (11)
Balmoral Primary School, Galashiels

My Dad

My dad takes me and Mum on holiday
My dad takes me to football
My dad takes us to a theme park
My dad takes me on a waterslide
My dad takes me and Mum shopping
My dad takes me on a train
My dad drives a bus
My dad does the gardening
My dad is always there
My dad holds a special place in my heart.

Craig Munro (11)
Balmoral Primary School, Galashiels

My Dad

He is always there for me
He never forgets me
He always cares for me
He's the world to me
I love the smell that comes from him
I love to be with him
I love the way that he carries on
I love the laughs that we have
I love the stories that he tells me
I love the way he inspires me
I love him to help with jigsaw pieces
I hope I can be as successful as him
I hope I'm going to grow like him
I hope I can be as good as him at rugby
I hope I can curl a football as much as him
I hope I can be as good as him at cricket
I hope I'm as cool as a cucumber, like him
Because that's the way my dad is.

Craig Hancock (11)
Balmoral Primary School, Galashiels

My Mum

My mum gives me a home to live in
My mum gives me a choice of food
My mum gives me a bed to sleep in
My mum takes me on holidays
My mum gives me clothes to keep me warm
My mum works her feet off looking after me
My mum cares for me
My mum trusts me
My mum believes me when I tell her something
My mum sends me to school so I can learn
My mum does everything to help me
My mum looks out for me
My mum has a heart of gold
That's why my mum is special
And holds a special place in my heart.

Natalie McMurdo *(11)*
Balmoral Primary School, Galashiels

Someone Special

If only I had determination
I wish I were strong, like you
If only I could be an entertainer and stunt master
I wish I had stamina, like you
If only I had the fitness and agility
I wish I were good at PE, like you
You inspire me Tony Jaa.

Tony Dale *(11)*
Balmoral Primary School, Galashiels

My Mum

My mum gives me lots of money
My mum gives me a bed
My mum gives me a holiday
My mum pays for activities at school
My mum does everything to help me
My mum gives me a pillow
My mum gives me food and something to drink
My mum gives me lots of clothes
My mum sends me to school so I can learn
My mum gives me help when I need it
My mum cares about me
My mum is always in my heart.

Nacisha Todd (11)
Balmoral Primary School, Galashiels

My Brother

My brother is the one I love
My brother is always there for me
My brother is so loving
My brother is also very silly
My brother is really smart
My brother always cares for me
My brother is the best brother in the world
My brother holds a special place in my heart.

Abbie Aitken (11)
Balmoral Primary School, Galashiels

Someone Special

My dad gives me confidence and courage
My dad helps me with my school work
My dad always makes me laugh and smile
My dad is always there for me
My dad is gentle, loving and caring
My dad is very kind-hearted.

My dad never puts me down
And you are never sad when he's around
My dad takes me on holidays
And I love to go with him
My dad is always nice to my friends
And jokes around with them loads
My dad is the best Dad I could ever wish for
I would never swap him for the world
He will always be in my heart
That's why he's my special person.

Carly Forrest (11)
Balmoral Primary School, Galashiels

My Heart

My dog, Riley, is so cute
He is there when I am sad
He comes to me when called
And holds a special place in my heart.

My mum is a special person
I would risk my life for her
She is so caring and loving
And holds a special place in my heart.

Mrs Andrew is the bestest teacher
She helps me so much
She's funny and kind
And holds a special place in my heart.

Mrs McClaren is so nice
I can tell her my problems
She will listen to my secrets
And holds a special place in my heart.

It's a good job I've got a big heart!

Andy Ross (11)
Balmoral Primary School, Galashiels

Someone Special

My dad inspires me by what he does
He helps me when I'm stuck
My dad inspires me when I'm stuck
He teaches me the rules.

My dad inspires me to treat people fairly
The way he treats me
My dad inspires me to be myself
To be proud of my achievements.

My mum inspires me to help others
She's always there for me
My mum inspires me not to give up
Always encouraging me.

My brother inspires me to be happy
Always cheering me up
My brother inspires me to share
Letting me borrow his toys.

My family hold a special place in my heart.

Ross Hume (11)
Balmoral Primary School, Galashiels

My Parents

If only I could have the courage
To be like them

If only I could have the strength
To be like them

If only I had the feelings
To be like them

If only I had the excitement
To be like them

If only I could face their challenges
To be like them

If only I knew exactly what I'd be facing
To be like my parents.

Callum McGuire (11)
Balmoral Primary School, Galashiels

Someone Special

E ilidh, Eilidh is my best friend
I t's like we can tell what the other is thinking
L ife is full of surprises when she is about
I t's as if she's got a big box of ideas in her brain
D oing things together is what I love
H appy memories, together forever.

Rebecca Russell (8)
Bishopton Primary School, Bishopton

Someone Special

You are special no matter if you are tall or small, fat or thin
No matter if you never win
You will always be a winner to me
And you will always be the one who is meant to be *special*
You always make me feel happy, when I am sad
And you never make me feel bad
You are a true friend and one day you will take me round the bend
To see a whole new world
You must remember everyone is special
Every single part of their hearts are *special!*

Kerry-Ellen Fleming (9)
Bishopton Primary School, Bishopton

Someone Special

Thomas, Thomas, plays football with me
When he does, he scores a penalty
When he scores the goals
He's like Paul Scholes
When he goes in goals
He saves them with his soles
When playing beside the motorway
He is a ball boy, he stops it getting lost in a convey
He's too young for a drink in the pub
He plays for Bishopton School Club
That's my brother, not my mother.

Jacob Bohill (9)
Bishopton Primary School, Bishopton

Someone Special

G reat gran, good
R eliable
E ducational
A ble
T houghtful

G enerous
R osy
A ffectionate
N aughty
S oft.

Alexis O'Reilly (9)
Bishopton Primary School, Bishopton

My Little Brother

M y little brother is full of laughter
Y esterday my brother was full of it

L ittle brothers are quite nice and fun to have
I love my brother, Callum and he loves me too
T imes my brother gives me kisses
T ime goes fast when we are having great fun
L ater, when it is darker, my brother and I watch a DVD
E very day Callum and I play with each other

B rothers are great fun to have
R unning and playing, football is his favourite game
O ut playing is really fun for him
T imes Callum does not like me
H eather and Callum are our names
E very time after dinner, Callum plays his games
R acing his cars is such fun for him.

Heather Munro (8)
Bishopton Primary School, Bishopton

My Sister, Gemma

My sister, Gemma, is full of love
I love her so much
She is really good at basketball
It's like she carries love
She's like the sun when it is hot.

Shona McCrea (7)
Bishopton Primary School, Bishopton

My Mum

My mum is the best in the world
My mum bakes fantastic cakes
She buys me nice things
She is kind and helpful
Mum likes to make me laugh when I'm feeling sad
That makes me glad she's my mum.

David Watt (8)
Bishopton Primary School, Bishopton

My Brownie Teacher

M y Brownie teacher is really brilliant
Y eah, she's a really generous person

B rownies have lots of kind people
R eally, I like Brownies
O ur trips are fantastic
W hen we go on trips, we have lots of fun
N ever will I hate Brownies
I   think my Brownie leader is wonderful
E very day we play games

T eatime is when I leave
E very time I go, my leaders are helpful
A t Brownies, we sing lots of songs
C oming to Brownies is great fun
H elping is normally the word my leader says
E veryone is nice
R eally, Brownies are cool!

Jordan Lamb (7)
Bishopton Primary School, Bishopton

Untitled

My pet dog is as cute as a rabbit
She helps me when I'm hurt
She is as funny as a clown
Her fur is golden like the burning sand
And as fast as a speeding bullet
She is as flexible as an acrobat
She is always there to play
She likes to jump like a frog, eat like a pig
She has teeth as sharp as a piranha
And is as stupid as a fur ball
This is my dog, Dixie.

Robbie Black (10)
Crown School, Inverness

Untitled

My crazy 80-year-old grandma
Is a very special grandma indeed,
She's climbed in the Himalayas,
Scuba dived all over the world,
Been in almost every country on the planet
And still has time to come home
To spoil me rotten and make her soup,
My mum says she's off her trolley,
But I'm glad she's my grandma and no one else's.

Alasdair McArthur (10)
Crown School, Inverness

Untitled

My someone special has got to be my unique Mum
Because she is kind and has so much time for me
She takes me places and looks after me.

My mum is kind, funny, energetic and fun
She has chocolate-brown eyes and long eyelashes
And midnight-black hair.

She is nice, but when she is angry
Her eyes go as red as a chilli pepper
She is like a speeding bolt of lightning
She always spoils me after, because she feels sorry for me
I love my mum
She's the best mum ever.

Natasha McAulay (10)
Crown School, Inverness

Untitled

My someone special is my fluffy dog, Ben
He is always kind to me
His fur is as golden as the burning sun
It's as soft as a newly fallen blanket of snow
He's as fast as lightning, he's funny as well
I love his crystal-blue eyes
I love Ben and he loves me.

Luke Henderson (9)
Crown School, Inverness

Untitled

My mum is someone special
Because she is always there for me
And she has sparkling blue eyes and has fuzzy hair
She is always wearing nerdy tops
She embarrasses me
And is always stealing the controller for the TV from me
But she always cleans up and buys the food for us
And I love her and she loves me
But who cares if she acts like a nerd?
She's my mum.

Euan Donald (10)
Crown School, Inverness

My Marvellous Mum

My marvellous mum,
She's short and has got blazing blue eyes,
Dark coloured hair and a short, pointy nose
And she's quite good at running too.
She acts like a taxi driver
Taking me to football training,
Cooks like a cook frying up my tea,
My marvellous mum is the perfect mum,
The perfect mum for me!

Blair MacLennan (10)
Crown School, Inverness

My Little Cousin

Jessie is my little cousin,
Who's very, very cute,
There's not another in the world,
That can do what she can do,
She looks like my uncle,
With chocolate-brown hair
And eyes that shimmer like the sky
She makes me laugh and she likes sucking things
And is very, very funny
So all of that together,
Makes her my side-splitting monster!

Bethany Foxcroft (10)
Crown School, Inverness

My Old Friend

My dog, Hamish, has a heart of gold
He's as black as a bat
As fluffy as a big grizzly bear
His nose is rough
His eyes are dark
He's as slow as a turtle
He could be as nice as a cat
He was a big dog, all full with glee
And he was the one for me.

Alison MacDonald (10)
Crown School, Inverness

My Dog, Sky

My dog, Sky, is extremely energetic
She can run quicker than a speeding bolt of lightning.
She is always there for me.
Once, we ran across the soft, golden beach
With the sun just peeking over the horizon
Reflecting on the sparkling blue water.
We sprinted back in pitch-black.
To our ginormous, dark-green tent
And we drifted to sleep.

Hamish Townshend (10)
Crown School, Inverness

My Cousin, Claire

My cousin, Claire
She has shining gold hair
Blue eyes like shining sea
As quiet as a mouse
As funny as a clown
Quicker than a speeding bolt of lightning
As clever as a super scientist
She swims like a fish
As gentle as a snakes scales
As scared as an insect
And she hates being untidy.

Erica Johnstone (10)
Crown School, Inverness

Wonder Mum

My mum is very special
I love her so much
She makes the house clean
And her cooking is so lush
She's never, ever mean
She's always happy and smiling
You should see the work I give her
It just keeps on piling!
My mum's the best
She cheers me up when I am sad
And if I get a bit naughty
She never gets mad
So, I really love my mum
And I do like my dad!

Catriona MacKenzie (10)
Crown School, Inverness

My Dad

My dad is the only dad you want
He's a funny one, but he's a grumpy one
Remember though, he's the only one
He's a sailor, he's a cyclist, he's the only Fiat buyer
He's got the smiley style and the baldy hood
Plus the nasty scar halfway down the nose
I always have and I always will
Have a Dad like him.

Finlay McCulloch (10)
Crown School, Inverness

Untitled

My sister, Shanelle, is horrible sometimes
But she can be funny and friendly
We have our share of fighting
But she is mostly nice
She has blue eyes, dirty-blonde hair
And she's short
My mum calls her 'Short Shanelle'
And my dad calls her a 'dangerous devil'
She likes to play with her dolls
And her favourite doll is Annabell
She is as slow as a slug
As slow as a snail
She is a tiny tot
But most of all, I love her a lot!

Chloe Cairns (9)
Crown School, Inverness

Someone Special

My mum is supportive, caring and gentle
She always spoils me, she is always kind
She has long brown hair, red glittering lips
Green apple eyes, clean, pearly-white teeth
She is happy, sometimes moody
She is funny, she cannot forget me
She is the best mum anyone can have.

Beth Urquhart (10)
Crown School, Inverness

Untitled

My friend, Danny
He is special to me
Because when I was in England
He was my first friend
I was so happy to have a friend
He has crystal-blue eyes like the sea
And chocolate-brown hair
He is as funny as a clown
He is as speedy as a bolt of lightning
As clever as a super-genius with shiny white teeth
Sweet and gentle
And he is as quiet as a mouse
And as tall as a giraffe
As clumsy as a blind bat
And he has big, banana feet
He's as lazy as an elephant
Eats like a pig and as noisy as a truck
He leaps like a cheetah
But he will always be my friend.

Bradley Millar (10)
Crown School, Inverness

Untitled

Sydney is special to me
Because she is caring
She is the funniest in the land
The most coolest person I've ever met
She is fabulous, she is fashionable
I adore her pearly-blue eyes
Her lovely chocolate-brown hair
With a tint of shimmering blonde
Her heart is made of the thickest and finest gold
She would never hurt me
She is loony
She is absolutely off her rocker
She is the sharpest tool in the box, that's for sure
But most of all, she is the bestest friend anyone could ask for!

Cheyenne MacLennan (10)
Crown School, Inverness

Cheyenne

C heyenne is my special friend
H er heart is golden like the burning sun
E veryone likes her and she's always
Y akking away about the most stupid, but funny, things
E very time I talk to her, I burst out laughing at her
N ever mean to me
N ever horrible to me
E very day sweet, nice and funny.

Sydney MacDonald (10)
Crown School, Inverness

My Mum . . .

My mum is always there for me
Every night and every day
She doesn't forget me for one minute, no way, no way, no way!
Her eyes are brown, with a hint of green
She's slick and thin and has a cheesy grin!
A face as smooth as silk
And gentle and kind with love in her mind
That's my mum!
She tucks me in my bed at night and sings a special song
Then says, 'Night, night' and turns off the light
I go to sleep real soon
That's my mum!
She's as quiet as a mouse
As she sweeps and cleans the house
She works all day, just cleaning away
Time for a break
That's my mum!

Andrew Calder (10)
Crown School, Inverness

Olivia

O livia is fun and funny
L ong, blonde hair,
I s lively and silly
V ery kind and helpful
I ncredibly strong
A happy chap.

Sophie Sibbit (10)
Crown School, Inverness

My Crazy Friend

My crazy friend, Sophie
Is kind, caring and very generous
Her favourite sport is running and skipping
She has chocolate-brown eyes
Like a chocolate bar
We always laugh at nothing most of the time
We also talk about who is playing with who
Her teeth are like pearls
And she is as bright as the beautiful sky
She feels like a soft, woolly blanket
She gives me any pencils that she doesn't want
And we play a lot of running games
At home and school.

Olivia Fielding (10)
Crown School, Inverness

Father

F unny, like a monkey
A s strong as an elephant
T he best dad at everything
H appy like a hyena
E xtraordinary, not like any other dad
R ough as a tiger.

Heather Kinsey (10)
Crown School, Inverness

Mum And Dad

You are special to me because;
You respect me
You trust me
You love me when I am down
You make me laugh and I love it
You give me presents on my birthday
You share stuff when we're in the car
You hug me when I fall
You stick up for me
You feed me
I love you, from Daryll.

Daryll Ann Hannah (7)
Duncow Primary School, Kirkmahoe

Grandma

You are special to me because;
You hug me after school
You play cool games
You take care of me when I am hurt
You buy me school shirts
You kiss me when I am sad
You don't know how much you mean to me
You always know what I see
I love you a lot
From Jordan.

Jordan Findlay (9)
Duncow Primary School, Kirkmahoe

Andrew, My Brother

You are special to me because;
You hug me after school
You help me when I am hurt
You play with me when I am lonely
You make me laugh when I am not feeling well
You take care of me when I am ill
You love me when I fall
Love from Stuart.

Stuart Slinger (8)
Duncow Primary School, Kirkmahoe

My Dad

My dad is really caring,
Funny and adventurous,
He's always really daring too,
He's never feeling blue.

He always does the best for me,
He always makes me happy
When I'm feeling down,
He takes me out a lot of the time,
To new places and experiences.

Cameron Scott (9)
Duncow Primary School, Kirkmahoe

My Special Papa

With my special papa, I have a ball,
When we go to the hall, he watches me play football,
Then we go up the town, I walk on the wall,
When I fall, he's always there for me.

Even if it's not my birthday, he'll buy me presents,
Not for my sister, but for me, yippee!
He'll always help me when I am down,
He never lets me down.

When he cooks me food,
I go straight to the pudding,
Except for the stew,
Then I go to the shop.

I go to his house every night,
He cooks me tea,
Then he helps me with my homework
And then we go out

And that's why he's the best papa ever!
Elinor Sioux Weir (11)
Duncow Primary School, Kirkmahoe

My Auntie Marion

You tell me jokes that make me laugh,
It's all because you are so daft,
You always say I am a star,
Then you tell my mum I will go far.

I've never met a lovely person like you,
You are so sweet and you always
Know what to do,
You make me lovely dinners,
It always feels like I'm a winner!

You always help me when I'm upset,
You persuaded my mum to get a pet,
You are loads and loads of fun,
That's why you're number one!

Stephanie Wells (10)
Duncow Primary School, Kirkmahoe

Papa

You are special to me because;
You take me to see lovely places
You let me see the chickens
You hug me when I am hurt
You take care of me
And you love me more than anyone
Love from Travis.

Travis Kelting (7)
Duncow Primary School, Kirkmahoe

My Dad!

My dad is lovely and caring
And never lets me down
But cheers me up
When I have a frown.

I could hug him
All day and night
And if I get a fright.

I love him
Even when he's gone
I'm still sleeping
I still love him.

He lets me count tags for extinguishers
It hurts my fingers
But it's OK.

I love my dad
He is lovely and caring
I love you, Dad
Just the way you are.

Hannah Paterson (9)
Duncow Primary School, Kirkmahoe

My Dad!

My dad is the greatest of them all
Yes, Dad, you're the best!
Dad, I love the things you do
And I've just got to say, 'I love you!'
Do the things you're always doing
But you'll support me whatever you're doing!
If you're not there, it's OK
So I would fight myself
To you, Dad, you help me keep in health.
Help me if you can,
Go and make me chips in the frying pan.
Eat up, he would always say
Big day you have a test to do
Everybody helps me on
School is not the best
Except the teacher, Miss Hunter
She's the best.

Dylan McNally (11)
Duncow Primary School, Kirkmahoe

My Cool Mum

She always makes me lovely dinners even if I'm glum
She always makes me giggle and I can't stop giggling
But she will always care for me no matter what
And she loves me no matter what
She is happy and always helpful
She takes me out to nice places.

Jordan Tweedie (9)
Duncow Primary School, Kirkmahoe

My Dad

My dad is helpful
My dad is kind
My dad is loving
And my dad is funny.

My dad is a truck driver
He shows me all the stuff
He makes me smarter
He makes me feel great
He calls me his mate
We have a joke
We have a laugh.

Ryan Gibson (11)
Duncow Primary School, Kirkmahoe

Tash, My Sister

You are special to me because;
You share with me if you have something and I don't
You help me if I hurt myself
You make me laugh because you're funny
You pick blackberries with me because you're an excellent sister
You take care of me if I am alone
You give me presents when it is my birthday
You love me because I am your brother
You play with me and you let me play with your games
You trust me if I say I am telling the truth
Love from Keenan.

Keenan Moss (8)
Duncow Primary School, Kirkmahoe

Téa, My Sister

You are special to me because . . .
You hug me before school
You hug me after school
You love me so much
You give me sweeties
You give me toys
You give me charms
You give me music
You play with me when I am alone
You do sits with me on the trampoline
You read me stories
You make me laugh a lot
You sing to me
You help me
You let me watch TV
You give me a kiss
Love from Erin.

Erin Ann Maloney (8)
Duncow Primary School, Kirkmahoe

Granny

You are special to me because;
You hug me when I'm hurt
You make me laugh when I'm lonely
You give me presents on my birthday
You love me when I cry
You feed me when I'm hungry
You help me with my work
You take me places when I'm bored
You share your sweets when I have none
You don't shout at me when I do something by accident
You care for me when I'm sad
You surprise me when I'm miserable
Love you loads, from Maisie.

Maisie Rands (9)
Duncow Primary School, Kirkmahoe

Mum And Dad

You are special to me because;
You help me when I get hurt or bullied
You hug me when I cry
You make me happy and you don't know how much it means to me
You give me presents
You always respect me
You help me when I'm stuck
You both are the best
Love from Josh.

Joshua Paterson (8)
Duncow Primary School, Kirkmahoe

Sophie, My Sister

You are special to me because;
You take care of me when I fall over
You play with me when I am bored
You feed me when I am hungry
You respect me once I've done it to you
You trust me when I've said something
You love me when I hug you
You help me when I get hurt
You share with me when I've got nothing
You play games with me
You hold my hand if we walk home
You buy me stuff
You look after me when I'm ill
I love you so much
From Molly.

Molly Kitson (7)
Duncow Primary School, Kirkmahoe

The Best Mom In The World

My guardian angel,
You love me unconditionally,
Always giving good advice.
My best friend,
The most amiable person in the whole world,
No one is like you.
You're an original,
Yet your beauty is seen in me.
You're a woman of God.
You instilled in me all the things I need to know,
To grow up to be a woman with integrity.
I don't say I love you enough,
But I truly do.
And if I had a choice, I would still choose you.
You're the best mom, friend and person,
A girl can ever ask for.
I don't deserve you,
But I have you,
And I thank God for you.

By the way, I love you!
Athena Cochinamogulos (12)
Queen's College, Bahamas

My Aunt

She was quite young,
But very wise.
She was always willing to help,
There to listen,
To guide
And to love.
She always told me,
'Live life to the fullest,
'Cause there's no promise of tomorrow.'
One day, she died a painful death,
Although the family prayed for her health.
In our hearts, it was not her time,
But the Lord always knows best.
She will be missed,
Always remembered.
Until that faithful day,
We'll get to see her in Heaven
And be a family once again,
Forever,
Amen.

Jerez Bain (17)
Queen's College, Bahamas

My Soul Sister

I found my soul sister
I found her by my side
She knows all of my dilemmas
And all the tears I have cried.

You are my soul sister
I just wanted you to know
Our love for each other
Helped us to grow.

Even though we've been through tough times,
We've made it through, I'll be there for you
Till the day of my death, sisters by soul forever
Till my very last breath.

My soul sister is like the rainbow
At the end of the storm, when life pulls
You under, I'll be the sun when there's
Lightning and thunder.

I always wonder if I deserve a friend like you
You seem to always know what to do.
You have such great wisdom and integrity,
A friend like you is truly a gift.

I will be here for you, till the very end
Just remember this: I will always be your friend.

Ashlee Dorsett (16)
Queen's College, Bahamas

The Way I Feel About You

Funny isn't it,
How love at first sight can seem so simple?
But there's much more background check to it.
Obviously, someone was trying to hide their feelings
When they said that,
Because it's not that simple.
I can't explain how much you mean to me,
The way I look at you and you look at me
And we both turn at the same time, as if we didn't, but we did.
I can't explain the feeling, but I know that it's you,
You make me feel like I can do better,
Just a simple glimpse of your face and I know that I could do it.
I hate you with all my guts for making me feel this way . . .
The way you tempt me with your looks, I can't think straight.
I'm losing my mind and the fact that you never speak to me,
Makes it even more frustrating.
People ask me why do I like you and why do you treat me this way,
But they don't understand.
I don't like you and I don't love you either,
I'm just on the verge of loving you and I'm getting there fast, too.
I hate you so much, that I can even cry and say it,
But the only thing that would come out, is broken fragments of words
Struggling to form sentences,
But they won't hide the fact that I will still love you
No matter what I say.

I wish I could shout your name really loud, but can't,
Because of what people might think.
So I must put my thoughts in this poem
So I could hear other's advice to direct me to the right path,
For I know that if I stay on the same path I'm on now,
Love just might kill me before I could fully understand it.

Onesha Adderley (14)
Queen's College, Bahamas

Someone Special

My brother is so special to me
He buys me whatever I want
And he is always there for me

He is so generous and kind
He makes me smile
He helps me with my homework
He has a brilliant mind and he's very kind

He cares so much for me
He really does
He spoils me like he spoils his cuz

He carries me out to parties
When I don't have a ride
He fills me up with dignity
Carefulness and pride.

Christina Pyfrom (12)
Queen's College, Bahamas

What A Special Lady She Was

What a special lady she was
She may be hard on you at times
But always showed love and affection
She was a humble lady
Never a wrongdoer
She was a woman of integrity

She was never rich and famous
Money wasn't an issue for her
She was always able to provide for her family
When times seemed to be difficult
She would pray, as that was habitual for her

What a woman of wisdom she was
She would always give you advice
As time passes by
She became closer and closer to me
As she was my best friend

Her time has arrived
And now it was time to say goodbye
Even though she is gone
She shall always be with me

RIP Grammy.

Zbigniew Dawkins (16)
Queen's College, Bahamas

Someone Special

She always found it hard to say, 'No!'
And is the most God-fearing woman I know.
Growing up with a house of nine,
Cooking, cleaning, all the time.
Raising passionately, nine children to feed,
Sewing up straw to pay for their needs.
Working till three over a hard sewing machine,
While her children lay snug in a room, so serene.
Gentle the heart, but hard is her soul,
Persevering day and night, at forty-something years old.
Struggling to find a few dollars for insurance,
In such a brutal world, she overflows with endurance.
Unbearable losses, unfortunate sorrow,
Yet thankful as can be, for today and tomorrow.
A smile here and there, sometimes even fear,
But oh, does she thank the Lord for her black and brown hair.

Moving time to time, struggling to pay rent,
But prays to the Lord to help her enemies repent.
Singing glory hymns to the black mountains high,
Always being thankful for the blue in the sky.
She praises the Lord for food, clothes and shelter,
Thanking the Lord for his compassion to help her.

As this is the life of Naomi Seymour,
My shield, my granny, for evermore.

Zhivargo Laing Jr (14)
Queen's College, Bahamas

Someone Special

My grandfather
Is so special to me,
Because of the way
He loves and treats me.

I love him more
Than silver and gold
And I don't care one bit
That he is old.

My grandfather
Helps me a lot with my math
And makes sure he leads me
Down the right path.

My grandfather
Calls me his superstar
And that when I get older
He'll buy me a car.

My grandfather
Has a very big farm
With animals
In a little barn.

I'll always love my grandfather,
No matter what
And his love for me
Is something that I can truly trust.

Jáydé Cooper (11)
Queen's College, Bahamas

My Role Model

My role model,
My sun in the sky,
Like my shadow that never leaves,
Always helping others, but never herself,
My guardian angel,
In all of the heavens,
My role model.

My role model,
Who I love so dearly,
So beautiful and so sweet,
We used to have fun together,
Until she got older and had to go,
My role model.

My role model,
So lovely and so amusing,
She is always there to help me in the bad times,
So much compassion and personality,
My role model.

Amber Stubbs (12)
Queen's College, Bahamas

My Heart's Flower

All I need in my life is her
She is the only one I can trust
She blooms brightly in the sun
She's the one who stands by me
There is no one quite like her
My heart would tear in two, if I lost you now or ever
She keeps her head held up high
But she smiles straight from her heart
She turns my nights into days
She seems me for who I am
She shows me what paths to take
Something tells me she's the one
She is my friend, my love, my flower
She is my special someone.

Samuel Jervis (17)
Queen's College, Bahamas

My Forever Friend

She taught me friendship
Before her, friends were ice cream sundaes sometimes
People who betrayed and lied always
But she was different
She knew when to laugh, love and listen
To me, friendship wasn't a necessity, but you proved me wrong.

We share the same loneliness, but we're never alone
I look up to you and you to me
Determined for each one to succeed
You know me, you see right through me
Even though we go through trials
But for the time spent together, it's all be worthwhile
You are my happiness, my sorrow, my love
My forever friend, Rhojai.

Jasha Winter (13)
Queen's College, Bahamas

My Best Friend

She is very beautiful
She makes me laugh.
My all in one
My everything and more,
She helped me out
When I was in need.

My best friend
Never asked for anything in return.
Gave all she could give
Love
Hope
Support
And happiness

My best friend
Watching over me until the very end,
Healed me when I was sick
Cheered me up when I was sad
Loved me through good and bad,
My best friend.

Danielle Farquharson (12)
Queen's College, Bahamas

Someone Special

He was resourceful and curious
He used to be artistic
He had to give it up
For his one and only
He saved her life
But lost his,

Just by saving her from that shark
Oh, how he fought it
But when he wasn't looking
It attacked him

He was so courageous
So very strong
He should still be here
He was the best!

Karah Hepburn (12)
Queen's College, Bahamas

Someone Special

The voice of people around the world,
The shoulder that's always there.
The giver to a person who has nothing,
The feeder to those who are hungry.
The person who cares without the credit,
The leader when no one follows.

The lover on rainy days,
The one who prays when nothing's wrong.
The cry of all people,
The drum of all hearts.
The smile that keeps you going,
The most contagious confidence.

The beauty of one who's lost,
The author of the word grateful.
The holder of the dream that lies within you and me,
Someone special!

Shea Stubbs (12)
Queen's College, Bahamas

Talented Person

He tried to pursue a music career
He was a very talented musician
And played seven instruments.
He taught a lot of people music
And others can now read it because of him.
He hardly ever got mad
And was never sad.
He cared a lot about other people's feelings
And always put others before him.
Then, at the age of nineteen,
He developed lung cancer.
He suffered for one year,
Barely hanging on.
A lot of people miss him,
Because he is now gone,
But his music will always live on.

Matthew Jesubatham (12)
Queen's College, Bahamas

A Special Person

She is determined
She would run till the end
I can tell her anything
I hope she can say
The same about me
Someone trustworthy
Holding secrets
Till the end
I know
She will help me
With what comes around the bend
She loves music
And she is very smart
I just want to tell her
She is a special person, without a doubt.

Manfred Ginter (13)
Queen's College, Bahamas

Barry Bonds

He's the king of home runs
He's the best hitter of all time
He beat the record for home runs a few months ago
He almost has 3,000 hits
When he does, he'll probably be called the best baseball player ever
He also has a good glove too
When I grow up, I'm going to beat all his records
You might think I'm crazy, but I'm not
I'm going to be the best baseball player ever
But what I'll do until I'm old enough to play,
I'll be admiring Barry Bonds.

Ian Banks (12)
Queen's College, Bahamas

The Man

A king among men is what he is to me
His skill in the kitchen is shown by his big round belly,
His voice is strong, when he speaks, people quake
I've know him all my life, so I don't even shake,
His eyes are slanted, but he sees all
Though he is not a giant, he still stands tall,
He carries himself with his own unique style
But I never know what he is thinking because he hides it with a smile,
In troubling times, he makes me glad
It makes me happy to call that man, my dad.

Christopher Chea (16)
Queen's College, Bahamas

My Very Best Friend

My very best friend,
Will tell you like it is.
The most important person in my life
Loving,
Honest,
Compassionate.
My very best friend,
Someone I could talk to about anything.
She taught me never to let anyone walk over me,
Always have my head held high.
She is my role model,
My motivator,
My inspiration.
She is always there if I need anything,
Taught me to be a young lady with aspirations and dreams.
I will love her always,
My best friend in the world.

Warel Smith (13)
Queen's College, Bahamas

Someone Special

Who is my someone special?
Many of you know her.
When I wake up at night,
An infection from a bite,
She is there for me.
So many ways to describe her,
Beautiful, tall, elegant,
Fun, fair, intelligent.
When I'm feeling down,
She's acting like a clown.
Rarely out of town,
Why? Because she's always around.
When I fall to the ground,
She helps me to my feet.
If I need any help,
Her advice I shall seek.
Who is my special someone?
She is always there,
Why, it's because Mummy truly cares!

Gabrielle Moxey (13)
Queen's College, Bahamas

Someone Special

My someone special
Is someone who is loving and careful
Always pushing me on day by day
Never stops making sure that I never lose my way.
My someone special
Is strong and never forgetful
Never forgetting important days in my life
Celebrating each event with me
Bringing out the best of each moment of every day as they go by.
My special someone
Always wants the best of the best for me
Always taking care of me, making sure that I am OK
Never leaving me alone, not even for a second
Because we never know what's going to go wrong.
My special someone
Is the one who has the most important part of my heart
All to themselves
My special someone is my father.

Adele Mangra (13)
Queen's College, Bahamas

Someone Special

Someone special,
The one that's always there.
Someone special,
The one to hold you near.

Someone special,
Will be there through thick and thin,
Even when you don't win.
Someone special,
Will eventually go away,
But we'll meet again someday.

They don't watch me fall,
We fall as one
And the love we share,
They know it all,
That someone special.

They probably don't know,
How much they mean to me,
But in this poem,
They shall see.
I love them more than they will ever know,
Our love will, like a river flow.

Amanda Phillips (13)
Queen's College, Bahamas

My Someone Special

My someone special is always there for me
From when I was an embryo in her tummy
From a tot and now a teenager
She is always here for me
Despite my behaviour.

I could never trade her for anything in this world
Not a diamond, a ruby or a pearl
No one could ever replace her
I thank God every day because He created her.

She is like my mood ring
Because she always knows how I am feeling
She tries her best to make me smile
And she does it quick
No one knows me better than this chick.

You probably know who she is
And why she is important to me
I always thank God
For making my mummy.

Raven Simms (13)
Queen's College, Bahamas

Someone Special

Is there someone special to you
Someone kind, caring and true
Someone who you will always love
Someone who is as pure as a dove?

For me, that someone, is my mother,
I am sure there is no other
Her brown skin and kinky black hair
Her way of saying, she'll always be there.

The generosity she has is contagious
Though the things she gives away are outrageous
Her cooking is, of course, the best
Her blinding smile, a cut above the rest.

Even when I'm in big trouble
She'll rush to my side on the double
The way she works so hard for me
Sometimes making me feel a bit guilty.

My mother is great, my mother rules
She is the world's most precious jewel
My love for her will last to the end
She's my role model, caretaker and friend.

Runako Aranha-Minnis (13)
Queen's College, Bahamas

Someone Special

The person who inspires me, is my mother,
She always had a way to make everything feel better.
When my dad died and I would cry,
She would hold me and say he is gone, just say bye.
I would always think, was she sad? Did she have feelings?
Why was I always crying and she wasn't even weeping?
What I did not notice, was that she was trying to be strong,
Strong like a rock in water when the tides try to push it on.
My mom is the best one in a million, like a gem lost at sea,
She is the only one that truly understands me.
Although my friends talk about how great their moms are,
I for one know, my mom is a star.

Kevin Farquharson (13)
Queen's College, Bahamas

Untitled

Did you know the dumbest dogs
You can imagine
Can still make you smile?
The dogs that chew everything
But always cheer you up
The dogs that jump on you
And mess up your white shirt
But always make you laugh
Yep, you got it
It's my dogs, Coconut and Tango.

Taylor Lightbourne (12)
Queen's College, Bahamas

Someone Special

She makes me laugh
And motivates me when nobody else can,
She helps me when I need it
And when nobody understands.
To me she is superwoman
And does what no other woman can do,
She helps me with my homework
And when I have the flu.
A mother, a daughter, a wife and a friend,
Her story, will it ever end?
She knows me perfectly
And I'll love her till the end.
The sweetest woman alive,
I've met her, I should know,
She carried me through life,
From birth until now.
Who is this extraordinary woman,
That makes me happy inside?
Yes, you've guessed it,
She is mine,
My mom that is.

Eboney Weech (14)
Queen's College, Bahamas

Someone Special

There's someone special in my life,
Do you know who it could be?
She's always standing by my side,
She's always there for me.

Nobody can replace her,
Even when she's not around,
To help me through my rough times,
To turn my frown upside down.

There's someone special in my life,
Do you know who it is?
She corrects all of my mistakes,
Because she knows what's best.

She is my hero,
My best friend,
My partner in crime,
Where do I begin?

There's someone special in my life,
Do you know who it might be?
This person is my mother,
Disrespect her, deal with me.

Amber Weech (14)
Queen's College, Bahamas

Someone Special

Known you since forever,
Started or began,
Loved you more than myself,
Before I learned to stand.

The little things you did for me,
Are greatly appreciated, of that I'm sure,
It couldn't get much better,
A love like yours so pure.

Never go away, please,
Stay with me, my love,
I'd choose you over life,
If push came to shove.

You and me together,
No love could compare,
Nothing is more perfect,
That the relationship we share.

Without you my life is barren,
Empty for all that sees,
Unusual and strange,
Like a stray without his fleas.

You're gone now, but that's OK,
'Cause you're with me in my heart,
I love you, Papa and remember,
We'll never be apart.

Ashleigh Russell (13)
Queen's College, Bahamas

Someone Special

My special person is my grandmother
The most immaculate person in the world
Every time I see her, she greets me
With a hug and a twirl
She always bakes muffins
They're like soft pillows of joy
At Christmas time she buys my brother lots of toys
She is always kind and worthy of my trust
If you want a good cake, seeing her is a must
She can sing really well
If you want to go to her concerts, you should
Patricia Bazard is her name
Kindness is her game
She won mother of the year in church
To find her you don't have to search
She lives in a small cottage
Baking muffins for her grandkids
She is no pest
She can withstand any test
That's my grandma, nothing less
That's my grandma, she's the best!

Denzel Bazard (11)
Queen's College, Bahamas

Someone Special

For my mother, strong and true
You know that I'll always love you
Thick or thin
Black or blue
If you ask you know I'll do
I see you work hard every day
You make the sadness go away
Understanding and commanding
I know that you will wait
For me to say what I have to say
So there's no such thing as late
You guide me and you show me to prepare me for the world
Then instantly all my confusion is unwrapped and uncurled
I know that you know I know you know best
You're the greatest mother of all the mothers
Better than the rest
Me and you, you and me
Depend on each other, as you can see
Without you, I would not even exist
You can fix the things I break and add a little twist.

Blanette Baltimore (11)
Queen's College, Bahamas

Mom

Your black hair
And brown eyes
Your soft voice
Sang me lullabies

You're very caring
And full of love
You get some help
From up above

Thinking out of the box
Is your thing
Your hugs and kisses
Are gifts you bring

You're very sincere
And loyal to me
Really how else
Should mothers be?

You've helped me always
When help was needed
Because of you
I've always succeeded

You gave me the most
Outstanding present
The gift of birth
Now isn't that pleasant

You've always held a place
Deep within my heart
And you should know
That you and I
Will never, ever part.
Shelby Carbin (12)
Queen's College, Bahamas

Someone Special

I really like the way
The way a person -
A special person
Knows how to make you feel better.

I have a special person
You should have one too
Someone for you to appreciate
And look up to.

Someone you will keep in mind
That special person that I have
I know I appreciate them
And look up to them.
Kennedi Bethel (12)
Queen's College, Bahamas

My Someone Special

My someone special that holds
A place in my heart
Is kind and loving
She is beautiful, outgoing
Outstanding and is number one.

My someone special
Has a key to my heart
She can lock it and keep it for herself
Or she can unlock it and give it to the world to share
But I know one thing
She will always be there.

She is my best friend when I'm alone
She is my teacher when I'm wrong.

My someone special is my mom
And this I really know!

Benjade Rahming (12)
Queen's College, Bahamas

Someone Special

There is someone special in my heart
I know there is no way we can be apart
I love her with all my might
Sometimes I have to hold on tight
She's been there for me for twelve years
We've laughed, played and even shared some tears
She is married to someone I know very well
They had another daughter, she's my sister, that's for sure
My love for her is so pure
She and he may argue and fight
But inside they still love each other
They've been married for 17 years straight
On their wedding day they ate off the same plate
We could travel the world together
And it wouldn't bother her
As long as we all are together
This person, for sue, is my mother.

Lauren Haven (12)
Queen's College, Bahamas

Best Friend Of Mine

The friend in you
Is always honest and true
The friend in you
Is who I truly value.

I honour your generosity
And kindness to me
Your humour and friendliness
And your overall personality.

The jokes we shared
The secrets we spread
The times we enjoyed
The times we laughed until we turned red.

Until the end of eternity
And the stars lose their shine
You'll be important to me
You'll be the only best friend of mine.

Savannah Newbold (13)
Queen's College, Bahamas

My Everything

Nothing in the world means more
Than having you for my own
Spending many days thinking about you
Always with you wasting hours on the phone

Nothing could ever replace you
Not shining silver or glistening gold
There's something about you
That I need your hand to hold

I belong with you
We were made to be
I'll say over and over
How much you mean to me

Don't ever forget, you're my pride
My love and the air under my wings
My happiness, you're the sun in my sky
Because you're my everything.

Ashley Fox (13)
Queen's College, Bahamas

Because Of You, I Love

What is love?
You showed me how to love -
How to care,
How to control freedom of speech.
You taught me how to stand up
For what I believe in
You gave me the tools to achieve anything
So I can be able to stand
On my two feet.
Just like in the beginning of eternity
Things of life
You trained me
How to walk
Talk
And most of all, believe in myself
Now I am able to be free
Because of you
You
My parents.

Brenizka Marshall (13)
Queen's College, Bahamas

Untitled

Thirty-six, thirty-eight, as I open my lock
I am thinking about my brother
It was such a tragedy that
We have the same mother

Tick-tock, I look at my watch
I think about his big, brown eyes
The way he looks when he cries
Makes me feel bad inside

Zip, zip, as I close my bag
I'm thinking of his soft hugs
The way I scream when he looks at me
And smashes a huge, black bug

Vroom, vroom, I'm in the car
On my way, I think of him
I love the way we are
Best friends.

Kirsten Klien (12)
Queen's College, Bahamas

103

Brothers

Brothers are there for you
To always help you get through
The hard times in life
That give you lots of strife

They show you how to do things right
Even if it's late at night
They do things to show you they care
Like buying new brushes for your hair

I don't know what the world would be without brothers
I can't imagine having another
They may make you mad
But then again, they always make you glad

Though I don't want this poem to end just yet
There's one more thing you want to know, I bet
My brothers are Neil and Chris
And I'm their only little sis.

Harmelle Davis (12)
Queen's College, Bahamas

Someone Special

Someone special to me is my sister, Shelbi,
She goes to QC and is fifteen
We love to crack jokes and play around
Whenever I'm in trouble from my parents,
She backs me up and I do the same
We love to go to the mall and Marina Village
We get Starbucks and ice cream
And then sit in the surf shop
Whenever Shelbi and I go to the mall
We hang out in the food court
Then we go to the movies
My sister loves the PS2
And she can't live a day without KFC
She is someone special to me.

Steele Curry (12)
Queen's College, Bahamas

Someone Special

Chasing butterflies in the yard,
Watching television all day,
Sleeping in bed all snug and tight,
Reminds me of the days,
When she was so small and tiny,
She would cry if she could not find me.
Just like another day in her life story,
Playing with her toys,
It is hard to believe she is only three,
Always trying to bother me,
Especially when I am watching TV,
I love her so much,
She is my sister, Asha Marie.

Ian Winder (11)
Queen's College, Bahamas

My Dream

My dream is to meet someone
Who has a good personality
My dream is to love this person
And maybe even marry this someone
My dream is for this someone to be very perfect
My dream is to find someone who is very sweet
Maybe even love to speak
This someone should be neat
This someone should be lovely
My dream is to find someone . . .

Antoine McKenzie (13)
Queen's College, Bahamas

Someone Special

Joanna was more than a friend,
She was someone special,
She cheered me up when I was down
And was always there when I needed her,
She'd come with me just to get my jacket
From the lost and found
Jojo as we called her,
Kept me and Ciara down to earth
She would barely make a sound
Yet you could find a smile on her face, no matter what
You can tell she's always happy, with just one look
And didn't care for many material things
Except for maybe a good book
But, what made her oh, so special
Was how she could put a smile on your face
Even if you were failing school
She'd have some way to make you smile
Since I sometimes needed a lift
I made sure I had her on speed dial
Since I moved away, I don't get to see her anymore
Which to me is lame
But I'll bet you, she's still the same.

Courtney Kalender (12)
Queen's College, Bahamas

Someone Special

She is that special someone that brings delight;
Who sparks like fireworks on a dark night!
She is lovable and caring, but alas!
She is sweet and sassy and definitely first class!
She's full of laughter and full of fun;
Tessa is my special someone who is number one!
She loves to go on the boat and swim in the sea
And then afterwards have a sleep over by me!
She's pretty, she's adventurous and brave too;
She's one of a kind and nothing like you!
She loves to eat different foods
And she always has her different moods!
She's an awesome person, that's for sure
And next thing I know, she'll be knocking at my door!
Just waiting for another adventure to come;
She's like no other, not even some!

Lianna Burrows (11)
Queen's College, Bahamas

Someone Special

I met this person the day I was born
She knows every colour paper I have torn
She has loved and cared for me
Since I was a baby.

But sometimes I get her upset
She screams when I come home wet
Sometimes she is very firm
But only because she is concerned.

She makes sure I am not up late at night
She shows how to do things right
She lets me hang out with my friends
For times that seem to never end.

Though I wish this poem would never end
I have to say goodbye my friend
There is one more thing I'd like to say
My person is my mother, by the way!

Déja Burrows (11)
Queen's College, Bahamas

My Special Someone

My special someone is black and white,
Very furry and is pretty small
Can you take a guess at who my special someone is?
She is my adorable kitty-cat, Jess.
Jess is definitely not a regular kitten; most cats, you see
Will be sleeping or digging through the trash, but not my Jess.
She can't stay still for a minute,
If she's not playing with the dog, she's playing soccer with me,
But only with a ping-pong ball, of course.
To me, Jess is special, because she's extraordinary.
Just like everybody else in the family.
She is the kind of cat, who never settles for the small stuff,
She's the most adventurous cat I've ever seen!
Jess is definitely one in a million;
I mean, how many cats do you know
That can hunt birds and snakes, flies and roaches,
But most of all . . . can pant like a dog, on command?

Kayleigh Dickson (11)
Queen's College, Bahamas

You're Special To Me

You're the best in this world,
You're the best there is,
You're the one who makes me smile,
You're the one I could kiss.

You're the best in this world
And I love you a whole lot,
To me, you're the greatest,
Because of the joy you bought.

You're the best in this world
And you've got a great heart,
You're as sweet as sugar and honey,
Or even a lemon tart.

You're the best in this world,
You're the one I truly need,
Because of all you've ever done,
You're the best indeed.

I've dedicated this poem to my dad
As he is a very special person to me.

Neha Kodi (13)
Queen's College, Bahamas

Someone Special

Baby Brianna
Is so dear to me.
When she laughs,
I'm happy inside.
She's a collection,
So I show her much affection.
She's adorable, not horrible.
I play with her,
Hoping she grows up,
The same way.
That's someone special,
Whom I care for happily.

Zinneá Smith (12)
Queen's College, Bahamas

Someone Special

Have you ever met someone special
Who is kind and loving?
Who is always there to give you a hand?
Maybe now and then
She tells an embarrassing joke?
Have you guessed yet?
Well, you're right
That person is my mom
She'll always have a special place
In my heart.

Danielle Grant (12)
Queen's College, Bahamas

Someone Special

Someone special I know
My mother and father
They care for me
Even when I'm not sick
They try to grant my every wish

They always buy me candy and cake
Sometimes so much, my stomach aches
They buy me gifts
Even when it's not my birthday

They always pray for me when it's time to rest
To me, my parents are the best
My parents are the apple of my eye
When they go away
I want to cry

My parents are surely as good as they sound
I know for sure
They are heavenly bound
Now that I am wrapping up
What I have to say
Salutations to all
And to all, a good day!

Deborah Johnson (10)
Queen's College, Bahamas

My Brother, Justin

Justin is my brother, like no other
He is my half-brother from another mother
That's why he is my half-brother.

He is 21 and my daddy's son
He takes me places and I see a lot of faces
A face on him and a face on me, that's
Why we were meant to be brother and sister.

He is kind, he is sweet and he is always on my mind
Like no other brother is,
He gives me money
And he is my big, cute bunny.

He finished college and has a lot of knowledge
He works for my dad and I am really glad
That he works there with him.

This is why Justin is my number one brother to the end
And my good friend!

Catherine Pyfrom (12)
Queen's College, Bahamas

My Mommy!

My mommy is my very special someone
She takes good care of me
Helps me with homework
And always loves me.

Even though sometimes I get on her nerves
Or me and her get into a fight
I can always count on her
To always be right.

When I'm in need of something
She always knows what to do.

So how does my mommy do all this stuff?
I really don't know
So, 360 days of the year
I do whatever she wants me to.

To repay my debt of
Thirteen years of expenses
Doctor fees and the most important
School fees.

This is why my mommy is
Sooooo special to me!

Jerez Rolle (13)
Queen's College, Bahamas

Someone Special

I know someone special,
Can you guess who it is?
She's not very tall,
Not very thin,
Not a superstar,
But I'll give you a hint.
She's loving, kind, caring and giving,
She works for herself,
To make a living,
She cares for her family
And is a loving friend,
She's always willing to lend a hand,
What inspires me the most,
Is how she cares for me,
Working two jobs nine-till-five,
Seven days a week,
Cooking and cleaning
And all that stuff,
Just because she loves *me* so much,
By now you should know,
Who she is,
She's my loving mother,
A role model and a best friend.

Anya Lewis (13)
Queen's College, Bahamas

Someone Special

Someone special to me
Sometimes he laughs, sometimes he cries
But it doesn't matter to me, because
I'm just happy to have him as my brother.

He gets on my nerves lots of times
But I know he's just trying to have fun
And when he gets mad at me
He always still forgives me.

We eat the same food
And we share the same room
But he's someone special
And he hasn't got a clue
It's my brother!

Tristin Hunt (12)
Queen's College, Bahamas

Untitled

My someone special is smart,
She always keeps her work balanced.
She never falls apart,
No matter what the challenge.

She is a hardworking queen,
But not much like the others.
She always thinks of me,
There's no question, she's my mother!

Aaron Chandler (13)
Queen's College, Bahamas

Grandma

My grandma is,
Loving,
Caring
And understanding!
She is
Sweet and kind,
Slow, but oh, so swift,
Special and of course, unique!
But most importantly,
She's my grandma!
Gentle and caring,
Soft-spoken and always understands!
Generous and always forgiving,
The one who always speaks her mind!
Christianity is always number one,
Family is always important to her too
And of course, precious in every single way you can think of.
Although I am far from her
And she is far from me,
She is my grandmother
And I am her grandaughter,
I still love her
And I know she still loves me!

Jordan-Tate Thomas
Queen's College, Bahamas

Special Someone

The special someone in my life, is God
Though mighty God of Heaven and Earth,
When I had fallen, he was there
To help me up
When I was lost,
He showed me the way
No friend I have, like him to trust.
My great God, He listened to my questions
And complaints
He loves me more than any fame
He hears my prayers
And changes my situation
In time of tribulation
I am His special child
And my heart desires to see
Forever happy we shall be.

Alexis Ferguson (12)
Queen's College, Bahamas

Someone Special

The day I met my grammy
She made me very happy
And gave me all lots of candy
She made me so very dandy.

She always used to take me to the mall
And used to pick me up when I used to fall
Whenever I'm with Grammy, I used to have a ball.

My grammy is so special
Because she gave me all lots of potential
She gave me all lots of courage
And used to make me some porridge.

My grammy was so much fun
She used to make me run
For an hour, until her turn.

Ruthvik Gowda (13)
Queen's College, Bahamas

The Way

I love the way you love me
And how you tend to care,
I love the way you stood by me
When no one else was there.
The ways you make me smile each day
Cannot be expressed in words,
The joy I feel is as sweet
As harmonised birds.
Thank you for what you did
Because you didn't have to do it.
I'm glad I found someone like you
Who could help me to get through it.
One thing I think is especially cute
Is the way you think you love me
As much as
I love you.

Jackheil Kemp (14)
Queen's College, Bahamas

The Closest Person To Love For Me

He causes me pain, but yet I love him
He's a complicated person, but yet I understand him
He's like a baaad boy, but yet I see the most good in him

He can be so kind, but at times, so cold
His attitude could get ugly, but his personality is so beautiful
Yes, he does get on my nerves at times, but I love him

He has never said one bad word to me
He always shows me he cares for me
I think this is close enough to love for me
Because I know that he loves me

I think he's wonderful
Not just because he is
It's because he's original
And his personality, there's no other like it

Honestly and truly, I love him, I do
And if he were here he would say he loves me too
I know this is strange . . .
But I know I'm so right
He's the closest person to love for me in my entire life.

Jasmine Nixon (14)
Queen's College, Bahamas

Her Ways

Loving, caring, sharing and welcoming
Are all descriptive words about this extremely special someone to me
Do you admire someone so much
You can picture yourself as them someday?

Well, yes I surely do
For that special someone is none other
Than the wonderful mother of my mother
My grandmother, not only my grandmother
But the lady I will always admire and greatly respect.

For she is incredibly thoughtful, joyful, faithful
Truthful, considerate, kind-hearted and really cautious
She is like my angel, always looking over me
For she ensures my every need is fulfilled
She's that particular person that knows what to say
When you're that lonely
Sad soul feeling like a dog whose bone just got taken.

Her love is one of a kind, for you can feel it in her presence
Her touch is one of a kind
For when she touches you, you can sense that generous,
Warm-hearted lady that lies within her
She will forever be that particular, unique lady I will always look up to
For I believe that someday, I will follow in her golden footsteps.

Shanier Dixon (14)
Queen's College, Bahamas

Better Half
(DEDICATED TO PRIYA)

Miles apart and still so near
My love for you shines far
You're my best friend, my sister and my counsellor.
I start my sentence, you finish it off
It's weird how we share the same thoughts
You're my soothing music when I'm depressed
You're my diary when I'm emotional
I trust you as I trust myself
You're my best friend, without a doubt
I hope to grow old with you by my side
You're truly my better half
In me, you'll always abide.

Apryl Pinder (14)
Queen's College, Bahamas

One and Only

She brings me joy,
She makes me laugh,
She loves me,
Even when I'm bad.
She helps me grow,
Physically and mentally,
Her love shines through,
For all to see.
Her heart is pure,
Pure as gold,
She is my life,
My one and only girl.

Patrick Paul (14)
Queen's College, Bahamas

Untitled

I think I'm in love, but
I'm not so sure since
I've met you, I've got this
Feeling deep inside, I don't
Know what it means,
But, I can take a guess
I'm glad that I got a chance
To feel this way with you
What I'm saying is true,
For better or worse,
We've made it this far,
To think that they
Would try to break us apart
After all we've been through
You make me feel,
As if I'm real
Together time after time,
Because of our love,
It would keep us together,
No matter what in this
World, together as one
Until the right time has arrived,
We will conquer it all.

Kalysa Carey (14)
Queen's College, Bahamas

Untitled

Do you have a heart? I think I do
I just never realised it until I met you
For a while, it was cute, just harmless discussion
Then we got serious, emotions flared
It was love so great, it could not be compared
But I was wrong, it wasn't love I felt.
She started not to stand me and I pretended not to notice
It was hard, because for years, she was my focus
Her hatred grew slowly, day after day,
I contemplated . . . when did it get this way?
It ended so sudden, no signs or anything
She left me with the words, 'You're not special!'
She was my someone special.
Devario Saunders (14)
Queen's College, Bahamas

Why Are You So Special?

I don't remember you
Maybe I never will,
But I still love you.

I know you love me
I'm starting to hate you,
But I still love you.

You're never around
Yet you're always there,
So, I still love you.

You never listen
I told you not to go,
Maybe I should forget you.

When are you coming back?
I can't wait forever,
Don't let me forget you.

Shannon Dawkins (15)
Queen's College, Bahamas

Sis

She stares at me with her auburn eyes,
She loves me,
I love her,
We share our lives together,
Total opposites of each other,
She is the comedian,
I am the serious one.
She might get annoying sometimes,
But, that is what I love about her,
I might be strict
And she may not like it,
That is just the way I show that I love her.
We are one another,
Just like yin and yang,
Beyond the fiery grasp of hate . . .

Elmer Lowe (14)
Queen's College, Bahamas

Just Like An M&M

He reminds me of M&Ms
He is my M&M
My favourite thing
Almost as if I am addicted.

He is sweet
And has a heart as big as the peanut inside
Even though the colour outside is fake
He is not.

All M&Ms are different
And he is like no one I've ever met before
He is never bitter
Or too sweet
He is just perfect.

Shaunna Pratt (14)
Queen's College, Bahamas

She's There

She's there,
When I'm happy.
She's there,
To make me smile.
She's there,
When I laugh.
She's there,
To stay a while.
She's there,
When I cry.
She's there,
When I need her.
She's there,
When I'm sad.
She's there,
When I need cheering up.
She's there,
When I'm a hopeless mess.
She's there,
When I feel alone.
She is . . . my sister.

Lot Barendsen (13)
Queen's College, Bahamas

Who Is He?

Who is he?
Is he a friend?
Or is he more than a friend?
I never thought our love ran so deep,
To a point where it can't be beat.
Gentleman or pretender runs through my head.
Who is he?
A gentleman!
He thinks of others before himself
And never brags or brings up his wealth.
I'm thinking that our love can't be compared,
To the feelings people say they feel in the air.
Although you might be very far away,
I know.
You know.
That our love will stay.

Azariah Miller (14)
Queen's College, Bahamas

Hero

Not many people can say they stared death in the face, I can
There is not much that I can remember from that night
But there is someone I can recall.

When your car rolls off a bridge, there's not much to think about
When life flashes before your eyes
There's no time to cry.

When your car is suddenly underwater,
You know you're going to drown,
You can only hope someone will be there
Or pray that this bad dream will disappear
As the water rises, so does your fear.

You hold your mother's hand
As if to say goodbye
To my astonishment, there was this guy
Without hesitation, without any doubt
He cracked my window and pulled us out.

I can never forget his face
The face of grace
An angel in disguise
A hero in my eyes.

Channah Toote (16)
Queen's College, Bahamas

133

Someone Special

Ever had someone special?
I sure did
He died when I was a little kid
He was extremely nice
And he sure loved Old Spice
Now that I'm older, I think of him all the time
In our front room, his picture always shines
This man I'm talking about is my uncle
After he passed away, life became a jungle
Even though he died in 1999
He is still missed in 2007
When I pass away, later in life,
I'll hope to see him in Heaven.

Alexandria Marshall (13)
Queen's College, Bahamas

Mattie

Her motto of life anything worthwhile doing is worthwhile doing well
Was a life lesson learnt, forever embedded in our minds
We have learnt how to love, live and how to care for others
Even our animals, as you told us,
'Do unto others as you would have them do unto you,'
Meditating on old times we all can remember,
The numerous numbers of licks we all got
But we saw when you hit us, it hurt you more than it did us
I thank God for the little and big things
You have done to accommodate us
Now I pray we all go to Heaven, where we will see you
Probably looking through a Talbot magazine or gardening
Whatever you're doing, we know it's to the best of your ability
I thank God for blessing all of us with you,
As our grandmother,
The time came when you became ill on us,
The woman who we thought would never die, was hurting
Nana, you've lived, you've loved, you've cared for us
And now it's time for you to rest.

Simone Munroe (16)
Queen's College, Bahamas

That Girl

First time I saw her was
Breathtaking
She had the most heavenly smile
Similar to an angel

Suddenly, she became that girl
I wanted to know who she was
Her best friend introduced us
And then I knew who that girl was

We talked on the phone every day
Feelings came
Told her how I felt
Unfortunately, she didn't feel the same

Tried to move on
But it was hard to face
The fact
That the love I was sending
Wasn't making it to her heart

She started off as that girl
With the heavenly smile
But who knew
She'd be that girl to break my heart.

Maxwell Glinton (16)
Queen's College, Bahamas

Untitled

The person I'll be writing about,
Is very dear to me,
I'll write it down in special form,
Just so you can see.

At first, when he was born,
It was love at first sight
And I said to myself,
'That's my brother alright!'

His love of everyone,
His love of me,
With his innocent cry,
You'll give him anything.

A toy, a book,
Pan or pot,
I'm so lucky
To have the brother I've got.

Finally,
I'll tell you right,
My special person,
Is Logan Cartwright!

Samantha Cartwright (12)
Queen's College, Bahamas

Dads

Dads are great
And they are never late
They're jokes aren't funny
Because they're out of date

But my dad is great
He's like a mate
And he always falls over
When we roller skate!

My dad goes to work
To earn lots of money
But to keep us all happy
He has to spend all his money!

When it comes to computers, he's no Bill Gates
But when it comes to other stuff, he really is great!
But there's something everyone will say about dads
And I've said it before and I'll say it again,
Just three words, which are . . .
Dads are great!

Charlotte Morris
St Joan of Arc Catholic School, Rickmansworth

My Dad

My dad is the best,
He is better than the rest,
He drives a big, black car,
He loves a laugh, ha-ha!
My dad, he is the best.

My dad, he's really funny,
He also loves my mummy,
He's always very caring,
But can be much too daring,
My dad, he's really funny.

My dad is my best friend,
But can drive me round the bend!
We play football, we play pool,
He really is so cool,
My dad is my best friend!

Connor McLaughlin (11)
St Joan of Arc Catholic School, Rickmansworth

My Dad

Dads are sometimes crazy
And dads are sometimes lazy,
But my dad's always happy, you see
And he means such a lot to me.
Dads are sometimes crazy
And dads are sometimes lazy
And when I'm feeling upset and sad,
He makes me feel fantastic and glad.

Liam Murphy (11)
St Joan of Arc Catholic School, Rickmansworth

A Poem About My Dad

Oh, Dad
You can be rather a father
Father is not old yet
But acts very old and grumpy!

Dad,
Why are you so lazy?
Why are you never giving up the TV controller?

Dad,
What are we going to do with you?

You don't do a lot for Mum!
Only when it comes to
A screw in the wall
But never a hoover around the house
Or a wash-up once in a while.

Dad, you know we love you really!

Lorna Walley
St Joan of Arc Catholic School, Rickmansworth

Daddy

Daddy, you're not just wrinkles
Your love is true and fair

Daddy, you're not just lazy
You're my big cuddly bear

Daddy, you're not just Daddy
You're the best there ever were.

Eleanor Fitzwilliam (11)
St Joan of Arc Catholic School, Rickmansworth

Why Did You Have To Go?

Without you, I feel so alone,
You've never come back, you've never shown.
Daddy, why did you have to go?
You left me alone, I felt so low.
Why did you leave our family and me?
Why couldn't you have let things be?
Now you've moved away to Spain,
My heart feels like it's down the drain.
Why won't you come back, Father?
I've missed you so much and your laughter.
So, please come home, Daddy,
Because without you, I haven't felt so unhappy,
I miss you, Daddy.

Jack Gibson (11)
St Joan of Arc Catholic School, Rickmansworth

Dad

I feel like the king of Heaven,
When I am with my dad,
That makes me so glad,
For one single moment,
The Earth stops spinning,
Everyone else starts staring.
Their eyes filled with envy,
But my dad is next to me,
So I don't feel bad.

Abbel Thomas (12)
St Joan of Arc Catholic School, Rickmansworth

Different Dads

Some dads are really embarrassing,
They think they're really cool,
The would go out like they look real good,
But act a total fool.

Some dads are really grumpy,
They just sit around all day,
If you asked them to play your favourite game,
They would just tell you to go away.

Some dads are really rich,
They have so much money,
They would buy you anything you want,
But I think that's quite funny . . .

Because my dad, well, he's the coolest,
He really is quite fab,
He loves me now and always,
So, I'm proud to call him *my* dad!

Elena Abbott

St Joan of Arc Catholic School, Rickmansworth

Why Do You Love Me So Much?

Girl who always needs her dad,
He does anything to spoil his girl.
He may have grey hair with half of it lost,
He may have a belly full of chocolate,
He may have a wallet full of love,
Mine!
He may have a shout that sends you to your room,
He may have glasses that see the lies,
He may snore like a big pig,
But that is why he is my dad!

Katie Alligon (12)
St Joan of Arc Catholic School, Rickmansworth

Dad

Dads are good fun!
They try to guide you into the correct footsteps
They look out for you
They love you, it's true
You may think they love at all
But when you fall, they will be there
To catch you, it's true
Deep down in your heart
You love them and they love you
It's true.

Steff
St Joan of Arc Catholic School, Rickmansworth

My Dad

The big giant who stalks the hall,
The man who will drive me to school,
This is the man who is the best,
Only one problem, he can't dress.

His angry voice will make you scream,
Like the women on the television screen,
He is the one who thinks he is right,
Until you tell him, that's not right.

He is the man who is always there,
But never buys you a teddy bear,
He gets you things you don't like,
Which could be a pink trike.

Now his name begins with D,
He is as angry as can be,
In the middle is A,
He is the one you will make you pay!

Joshua Zeoli (12)
St Joan of Arc Catholic School, Rickmansworth

My Dad

My dad is amazing
In many, many ways:

He loves to eat chocolate,
But still is as slim as a stick.

My dad likes to read, but not that much
He prefers to keep fit and healthy.

He likes to watch TV,
But is still as busy as a bee!

I love my dad
Cos he's always there for me!

Ciara Warburton (12)
St Joan of Arc Catholic School, Rickmansworth

Dad

Let's take a look at Father,
A man that is full of laughter.
He sits and hugs me on the sofa,
Man, he can be such a loafer!
Mine's tall,
But even he can fall!
Hear him getting in the shower,
Yeah, he thinks he's got the power!
But even if he makes you sad,
Just remember, he's your dad.

Louisa Goad (12)
St Joan of Arc Catholic School, Rickmansworth

Make A Wish

Does he love me?
Sometimes I think
Leave me in the dark
And comfort your favourites
Like being in a shadow
Of a shining bright light.

A mountain to climb
To reach your heart
Is it cold as ice
Or hot like a fire?
Will I ever find out
Where your footsteps lead me?

Marry your books
You always tell me
My social life is fading
Bit by bit
Why is this happening?
I don't know
Maybe it is because of you.

Friends will deceive you
You always say
Friends will lie
You always think
Have you ever had a friend
To know what it's like?

Does he love me so?
Sometimes I think
Leave me in the dark
And comfort your favourites.

Here comes a shooting star
Make a wish

Time is fading
Think very carefully
I wish I were the mountain
That grows in your heart.

Pearl Narh (12)
St Joan of Arc Catholic School, Rickmansworth

You Are

You are the one that brightens my dad,
I wish that you never go away,
For I will miss you in that way,
That only I can.

You are the one that shows me how,
You show me things that make me go, 'Wow!'
Because you are the one that will allow,
My dad to go well.

When I fall over, you are there,
To pick me up and ruffle my hair
And no matter what, you will always care,
You are my dad.

Thomas Fortey
St Joan of Arc Catholic School, Rickmansworth

Dads Are Different!

Dads can be small, tall, fat and thin,
They always think they have to win.
They stare at you from time to time
And make you think that dad - he's mine.

Some people say my dad's so silly,
But I know he's just made of jelly.
He's always there, right by my side,
When I'm in trouble, he's so kind.

Some dads will always look really unpleasant,
In fact, mine looks just like a pheasant.
So, all dads are quite different,
But they are always going to be there to listen.

Sophie Peters (12)
St Joan of Arc Catholic School, Rickmansworth

Daddy

I'm always by your side, Daddy
And you're always by mine,
You walk with me wherever I shall go,
I skip, you skip,
I jump, you jump,
I hop, you hop,
I'm always by your side, Daddy
And you're always by mine,
We're a team at no rest.

Saskia Smith (12)
St Joan of Arc Catholic School, Rickmansworth

Dad, I Love You

Dad, you're ever so loving,
Always giving me kisses and hugs,
I'm your little mini you!
But sometimes we act like we're mugs.

How come you're so warm-hearted?
You care for everyone but yourself,
But you should treat yourself, every now and then, Dad,
Otherwise, it's not good for your health.

Your hugs are simply the best!
There's a spark as soon as we touch!
Daddy, there is only really important thing,
It's that, *I love you so much!*

Jessica Hatton (12)
St Joan of Arc Catholic School, Rickmansworth

My Dad

I love my dad, he is the best,
Better than all the rest.
He loves his sports, especially running,
He also is very funny.
The man is great, he is so kind,
He is in his own piece of mind.
I love my dad, he is the best,
Better than all the rest.

Rhys McCafferty (11)
St Joan of Arc Catholic School, Rickmansworth

Dad

God took:
The strength of a giant
The calm of a quiet sea
The patience of a saint
The happy buzzing of a bee

The brilliance of a book
The brains of a nerd
The silliness of a clown
And the nicest voice I've heard

You make me smile
You make me laugh
You are the best
And as tall as a giraffe

God knew His creation was complete
He knew there was no more to add
He knew he would have a great life
And so He called him . . . Dad!

Michaella Fennell (12)
St Joan of Arc Catholic School, Rickmansworth

Dad

My dad is loving in every way
He tells me he loves me every day
He's funny and annoying all in one
Like making sure my homework is done
He's as brave as a lion
And snores like a bear
He's tall and good looking, even without hair
He tells me to always do my best
And always have a go, even if the answers to the questions
I don't think I know
He's always there for me no matter what
And I think I've got the greatest Dad of the lot
He has a big heart, as big as the moon
And always puts me first
He always says he's proud of me
And that his heart could burst
So, when I talk about my dad, is it any wonder
That I have a smile from here to here
And glad his wings I'm under!

Sophie Williams (12)
St Joan of Arc Catholic School, Rickmansworth

My Dad

Every kid needs a father
When happy or sad
With a father things are never quite bad

My father is football mad
But very fashion sad
He is energetic
And sometimes when asked to do things, is very pathetic

His tummy is big and cuddly
He's always on a diet
And when he's hungry, he becomes ever so quiet

I feel so lucky to have him
To me he is the only one
And I'm so proud to be his son

He is funny, kind and sometimes strict
But I wouldn't want him to be another mix

In the future, one day
I'd like to be like him
I pray.

Stephen Richards (11)
St Joan of Arc Catholic School, Rickmansworth

Daddy, I Miss You

Something's missing in my house,
It's more than a television, it's more than a mouse,
It's someone special, someone, but who?
Daddy, oh, Daddy, I miss you.

Something's missing in the frame,
Something that never will be the same,
Something that used to give me something to do,
Daddy, oh, Daddy, I miss you.

Something's missing for me to follow,
Now it makes my heart hollow,
Something that makes me cry a lot too,
Daddy, oh, Daddy, I miss you.

Something's missing in my heart,
We should have never been apart,
Something missing, something true,
Daddy, oh, Daddy, I miss you!

Sofia Knowles (12)
St Joan of Arc Catholic School, Rickmansworth

What Would I Do Without My Daddy?

My daddy, well, what can I say?
I love him more than anything
He is better than the rest.

I know he is getting white hairs and wrinkly,
But my daddy is still better than the rest.

You're forgetful, yes!
But my daddy is still better
Than the rest.

Daddies don't grow old,
Instead they age and age,
But oh no, my daddy
Is still better than the rest!

Marie Chatterton
St Joan of Arc Catholic School, Rickmansworth

Dad

My dad is always there,
He might swear,
He's as strong as a bear,
He's very rare,
He's the bestest dad that anyone could have
He's very funny,
But has no money,
He works so hard and never has a break,
I wish the world had more dads his way.

Daniel Edson
St Joan of Arc Catholic School, Rickmansworth

The Thing About Dads

The thing about dads
Is that when they're a mess
Their heads have gone funny
And their brains become less
They still like to know they're the best.
The thing about dads
Is that when they've grown old
Their knees have gone creaky
And they've got much less bold
They still like to know they're the best.
The thing about dads
Is that when they're less lean
They start writing memoirs
And liking broad beans
They *still* like to know they're the best.

Isabel Langdale (12)
St Joan of Arc Catholic School, Rickmansworth

155

My Dad

My dad's name is Paul
He thinks he's very cool
He's also not very tall
Or very small

My dad loves his machines
Or eating lots of baked beans
My dad wears a lot of green
When he is mean

He likes to ride motorbikes in the mud
Rather than going down the pub

My dad thinks he's funny
Playing jokes on my mummy
When he acts dumb
He could be a little glum

That's what my dad is like.

George Gwinnell
St Joan of Arc Catholic School, Rickmansworth

Please Don't Wake Me Up In The Morning, Dad

Please don't wake me up in the morning, Dad
If you do, I will be ever so sad
You sound to me like a stereo machine
Your quiet voice is like a scream
The way you pull the covers off my bed
It's so cold, it feels like our garden shed
So, please don't wake me up in the morning, Dad
I'm sure I'll get up in my own time
Because when you wake me up
It doesn't feel like rise and shine!

But on the weekend when I have got loads of energy
And I am ready to go
You are so slow
So, please wake me up in the morning, Dad
If you don't, I will be ever so sad!

Rachel Barnwell
St Joan of Arc Catholic School, Rickmansworth

Where's My Dad?

Where's my daddy?
Is he in bed, at work?
I don't know.
I need to look for my daddy
He raises me high and he wrestles me
He tickles me and I laugh
Then he has to go to work
I miss him
Then, Daddy comes back
And he makes my tea
And soon it's bedtime
Then he goes away
Where's my daddy?
Upstairs, downstairs or anywhere
Where could Daddy be?

Luke Parry (11)

St Joan of Arc Catholic School, Rickmansworth

I Love My Daddy

I love my daddy,
Wherever he may be,
If he's gone or not
And I know he loves me.

Still I look for him every day
And if he comes, he would stay,
But now you're gone and I'm so sad,
I wish you were still here with me.

I see you every day,
But now not, because you see,
I really miss you every min,
I wish you could still be here with me.

I know you're with me every day,
But I want to hug you so very much,
So I dream about you every day
And imagine you're here with me.

Now I see you, because you're here with me,
But we much *never* say goodbye,
Because you're anything but a dream,
I miss you so very much.

Anna McConnell (11)
St Joan of Arc Catholic School, Rickmansworth

Someone Special

Someone special to me
Is someone who has stood by me throughout my life
Someone special
Is someone who can cheer me up
Even when the sky isn't blue
But even when you're alone
They always think of you.

My dog, Fawn, was a family treasure
Someone who can bring anyone pleasure
Her gentle eyes, even for a dog, so big in size
She didn't need companionship
For Fawn and the stars were already friends
Always there when you need her
Always sleeping by the door on cold winter nights
Her soft, furry coat kept you warm when you hugged her
But also kept her warm too
But now she is gone
I feel someone has turned the sky green
And the grass blue
I also feel nobody will miss her
The way I do.

Rachel Boyd (11)
Stonehouse Primary School, Stonehouse

My Friend, Layna

My friend, Layna
Is nice to me
Has brown eyes and long nails
She likes to play football
She doesn't like netball
I think she is funny.

My friend, Layna
Is kind to me
Has a big smile
She loves eating pizza
She really doesn't like mushrooms
She always makes me laugh.

My friend, Layna
She looks nice
Has long brown hair
She likes gymnastics
She hates SpongeBob SquarePants
She makes me sad when she doesn't play with me.

Chloe Jarvis (7)
Stonehouse Primary School, Stonehouse

My Big Cousin, Lindsay

My big cousin, Lindsay
Is very funny
She has red hair and freckles
She really likes playing the piano
But she does not like boys who are annoying
She really makes me laugh a lot.

My big cousin, Lindsay
Is good at the piano
She has green eyes
She likes eating chocolate
But she doesn't like mushy peas
She makes me happy.

My big cousin, Lindsay
Trusts me
She has lovely curly hair
Most of all, she likes playing netball
But she hates not going to Girls Brigade
Sometimes she makes me annoyed
Because she leaves me out.

Kirsty Rae (7)
Stonehouse Primary School, Stonehouse

My Little Sister, Emma

My little sister, Emma
Makes me laugh
She has shiny brown hair
And has light skin
She likes playing outside
But doesn't like tidying up
She makes me very cheerful.

My little sister, Emma
Cares about me very much
She likes eating sweeties
But doesn't like football games
She makes me full of energy.

My little sister, Emma
Loves me very much
She loves her family
But hates wearing jackets
She makes me angry
When she messes up my room.

Layna Stewart (8)
Stonehouse Primary School, Stonehouse

My Little Brother, Isaac

My little brother, Isaac
Can make me smile a lot
He has blue eyes
He loves to pull things off the table
Isaac doesn't like it when my mum goes out
I think he's very cute.

My little brother, Isaac
Tries to sing
He has blond hair
He likes to try to climb out of his cot
Isaac sometimes doesn't like his food
Isaac can make me laugh in bed.

My little brother, Isaac
Tries to pull my hair
The nicest thing about him is
He looks like me
Isaac likes to annoy my dad
Isaac hates to go to sleep
Isaac really annoys me when he screams his head off!

Amber Ross (8)
Stonehouse Primary School, Stonehouse

My Little Sister, Ailsa

My little sister, Ailsa
Is very special to me
She has blonde hair to her shoulders
She likes being at nursery
But doesn't like going to bed
I think she is very funny.

My little sister, Ailsa
Is very cuddly
She is quite tall
She likes rolling on the grass with me
But does not like getting told, 'No'
She makes me laugh.

My little sister, Ailsa
Loves me very much
She is very cute
She likes running in the house
She does not like bumping her head
She sometimes makes me angry
When she comes into my bedroom.

Rhuari Robb (7)
Stonehouse Primary School, Stonehouse

My Big Sister, Kimberly

My big sister, Kimberly
Is very funny
She is tall with brown hair
She really likes films and cats
But doesn't like football
I think she is especially nice.

My big sister, Kimberly
Shares things with me
She has lovely blue eyes
She likes to wear fancy shoes and clothes
But doesn't like scary films
She makes me laugh all the time.

My big sister, Kimberly
Is really kind to me
The nicest thing about her is her hair
She loves our baby sister, Rachel
But really hates wrestling
She makes me happy
When she takes me swimming.

Lauren Blair (8)
Stonehouse Primary School, Stonehouse

My Friend, Shaun

My friend, Shaun
Makes me laugh
He has black hair
He really likes playing football
But doesn't like washing up
He is very funny.

My friend, Shaun
Is really smart
He has nice brown eyes
He loves playing with his other friend, Jack
But hates to tidy his room
He makes me smile a lot.

My friend, Shaun
Can be silly sometimes
I like his happy face
Best of all, he likes his Nintendo DS
But really hates getting up on school days
He makes me happy when he tickles me.

Craig Dunn (8)
Stonehouse Primary School, Stonehouse

My Baby Cousin, Ellie

My baby cousin, Ellie
Is very cute
She has very long eyelashes
And she likes cuddly toys
She doesn't like going to bed
She makes me feel happy.

My baby cousin, Ellie
Makes me laugh
She has a very cheeky grin
She likes train sets
She doesn't like going for walks
She sometimes does silly stuff.

My baby cousin, Ellie
Tries to catch my toes
She is so sweet and pretty
She loves her food
But doesn't like getting up in the morning
She will always be my favourite person.

Caleb Fleming (8)
Stonehouse Primary School, Stonehouse

My Dad, Philip

My dad, Philip
Is kind at home
He has dark hair and a freckly face
He tells funny jokes
He hates tidying up
He makes me laugh.

My dad, Philip
Takes me down the park
He has blue eyes
And he likes to play
He does not like shouting
He smiles a lot.

My dad, Philip
Loves to have fun
I like it when he smiles
He likes giggling
He hates being annoyed
I love my dad.

Sarah Baxter (7)
Stonehouse Primary School, Stonehouse

My Big Brother, Ewan

My big brother, Ewan
Helps me learn football
He has long black hair and is tall
My big brother likes playing on the Nintendo DS
He doesn't like doing homework
I think he is adventurous.

My big brother, Ewan
Teaches me karate
He has great taste in music
My big brother likes going on adventures
He doesn't like hurting nature
Ewan makes me laugh.

My big brother, Ewan
Buys great birthday presents
The best thing about him is his long hair
He likes playing football best
Ewan hates causing an argument
Sometimes he makes me yell at him
When he annoys me.

Shaun McTaggart (8)
Stonehouse Primary School, Stonehouse

Untitled

My little sister, Becca, is very small
She is not like me because I am tall
In her dancing show she was a mermaid from under the sea
And this is why I am writing about her
Because she is special to me.

She has shiny blue eyes
When you look into them
You might get a surprise
And her long, blonde hair is very fair
And we always need to share.

She makes me happy
But she likes to be snappy
But when she is good
She can still go in a mood.

Kendal Murdoch (10)
Stonehouse Primary School, Stonehouse

Louise

L ouise is as sweet as cherry blossom
O h, I'm so lucky I've got her
U nderneath in my heart
I s the love of the special friend
S he's my friend
E verybody likes her, she's the bestest friend anyone could have.

Angel Yuill (9)
Stonehouse Primary School, Stonehouse

Untitled

My mum is very small
And she likes to go shopping at the large mall
She has got blue eyes
But she really hates pies.

My mum is hilariously funny
And she gives me loads of money
My mum is really kind
But my mum's mind is really hard to find.

My mum is very cheerful
And always helpful
Even though she is really mad
But when she sees me, she is really glad.

Cara Dawn Loudon (10)
Stonehouse Primary School, Stonehouse

My Dad

My dad is a very special man
He makes money in his fruit van
When I play, he's always there
Win or lose, he doesn't care
Because my dad is my number one fan.

David Ferguson (11)
Stonehouse Primary School, Stonehouse

My Brother, Douglas

D aft, funny, he teases me
O ften annoying, sometimes we fight
U ntil I remember, he is a
G ood guy who makes me
L augh out loud and is
A lways there to keep me
S afe and sound.

Fiona Baxter (11)
Stonehouse Primary School, Stonehouse

Untitled

My gran has grey, wispy, curly hair
She loves all fruit, her favourite is a pear
Her skin is old, it is bold and full of wrinkles
And when I come in, her eyes just twinkle.

My gran gives me lots of shiny money
She is full of jokes and very funny
She tells my mum that my behaviour is very good
She cooks me lots of tasty food.

When she talks about dying, she makes me sad
Sometimes when I do naughty things, she calls me bad
She is the best
Out of all the rest!

Alan Gordon (9)
Stonehouse Primary School, Stonehouse

Untitled

My gran tells jokes that are funny
Best of all, on Saturday she gives me money
Her face is awfully wrinkly
But her eyes are still twinkly
When I come she is very helpful
And also very hopeful
She helps me when I am hurt
When I am lost she always finds me
Even when she shouts at me
She still has a heart of gold
When I touch her, she is always cold
She is always happy
And she sounds a bit snappy.

Mark Carruthers (9)
Stonehouse Primary School, Stonehouse

Katie

K atie shares secrets with me
A ctually, we have been friends since playgroup
T oday she helped me when I fell
I think she's kind and helpful
E very playtime she plays with me, it makes me very happy!

Amy Whiteford (8)
Stonehouse Primary School, Stonehouse

Untitled

Simrut, Simrut, has jet-black hair
His favourite snack is salt, sour and vinegar crisps
He has multicoloured clothes
He is smart and he likes to take part.

He is cool, but sometimes he can be a fool
He gives me shiny money, then I give him honey
He is very nice, but he puts cold ice in the rice.

Simrut is very good
But he puts me in a big mood
He hates pickles very much
He tickles me till I start to cry
Now I'm going to put an end to this poem
My very best friend.

Joravar Singh Uppal (10)
Stonehouse Primary School, Stonehouse

Mummy

M y mummy is so special to me, I love her lots and lots
U s two are very happy together
M y mummy will never forget me, because I am so special to her
M y mum takes me lots of places, like ice skating, swimming and shopping
Y ou're the best mum anybody could ever have.

Ainsley Taylor (8)
Stonehouse Primary School, Stonehouse

Untitled

My cousin, Jamie, is very tall
Though he is tall, he can definitely kick a ball
He has spiky brown hair
Jamie is as cuddly as a bear.

To me, he is very kind
And he has a creative mind
Jamie is very clever
He has me as a cousin forever and ever.

My cousin, Jamie, is very glad
I cheer him up when he is sad
He tells me jokes which are funny
And when I am hungry, he gives me honey.

Blane Notman (9)
Stonehouse Primary School, Stonehouse

My Mum

My mum is lovely
And she is soft and cuddly
I love my mum
I like my mum lifting me
She has brown hair and earrings
And she has got blue eyes.

Chloe Logan (6)
Stonehouse Primary School, Stonehouse

Untitled

My friend, Alan, is very tall
He is taller than a brick wall
He has shiny blue eyes
Just like tiny little flies.

He is kind and really nice
He is quieter than three mice
He hates me when I show him a nut
He likes to sit in his hut.

He makes me welcome and glad
Sometimes he drives me mad
But he makes me cool
And likes pushing me in his pool.

Blair McKay (10)
Stonehouse Primary School, Stonehouse

My Gran

My gran is like sweets
She is so friendly
She takes me to the park
I go to the sweet shop
She buys lots of sweets
She's happy, snuggly, cuddly
She is spectacular and she is joyful
My gran is a happy sweet
Brilliant, funny, great and excellent.

Jack Bell (7)
Stonehouse Primary School, Stonehouse

Untitled

My friend, Chelsea,
She gives me lots of shiny money
And has a bunny
But she is hilarious and very funny.

My friend, Chelsea
Has fair brown hair
When I go round
She has always found her way around.

My friend, Chelsea
She is very happy
But she wears a very stinky nappy
But she always cares and shares.

Kimberly Blair (10)
Stonehouse Primary School, Stonehouse

Craig

C   raig lets me play with him at playtime
R   ed is his favourite colour
A   nd he is great fun to play with
I   really like Craig
G   lorious times I've had with Craig.

Scott Wilson (9)
Stonehouse Primary School, Stonehouse

Untitled

My best friend, Shannon, has a lovely face
Sharing a room with her is the best place
Shannon also has beautiful green eyes
If there was a competition, she'd win the prize.

Shannon is a great secret keeper
Our friendship just gets deeper and deeper
Shannon is so very smart
Our friendship can't be torn apart.

Shannon makes me feel very cared
None of our secrets have ever been shared
Now my poem must come to an end
About my lovely, kind, best friend.

Jasmin Vlassis (10)
Stonehouse Primary School, Stonehouse

Dad

D ad gets me toys on the way home from work
A nd takes me to really fun places
D ad's a very special person to me
   and he showed me how to tie my laces.

Lewis Davies (9)
Stonehouse Primary School, Stonehouse

Untitled

My dad is like dark chocolate
Because he is cool and sweet
My dad is like hot coffee
Because he is a treat
My dad is like a big, warm bed
Because he is soft as well
My dad is like the colour grey
Because when we go fishing he is a camera flash
My dad is like a harbour seal
Because he is a brill diver
My dad is like a pair of shorts
Because he is hot and funky!

Eva Margaret Wilkie (7)
Stonehouse Primary School, Stonehouse

My Sister

My sister is like noodles
Because she is warm and great
My sister is like orange juice
Because it is delicious and is smooth
My sister is like a bed
Because it is comfy and cosy
My sister is like pink
Because it is bright and cheerful
My sister is like puppies
Because they are small and cute.

David Beckett (7)
Stonehouse Primary School, Stonehouse

My Dad

My dad is like fish
Because it is very tasty and great
My dad is like Coke
Because it is my favourite drink
My dad is like a bed
Because it is my favourite piece of furniture and it is comfy
My dad is like brown
Because it is the colour of the horse I ride
My dad is like a leopard
Because it is a very fast animal and he runs very fast too
My dad is like my very lovely top
Because he is cool and funny.

Leiha Martin (7)
Stonehouse Primary School, Stonehouse

My Gran

My gran is very special
Last month she got a new kettle
She comes to babysit when my mum's away
But she doesn't come up every day
We sometimes play Snakes and Ladders
She gets me the best presents
She knows everything, from maths to pheasants
I love my gran.

Ross Wilson (9)
Stonehouse Primary School, Stonehouse

Always In My Heart

My uncle Robert, is my very best friend
He helps me when I fall
He lets me go on his shoulders
If my legs are in pain
He's the funniest person I know
He supports Man United
He lives at Boghead
I help him with the sheep
And the cows too
He's the most special person I've ever had
I love him so much
He's always in my heart
My uncle Robert.

Rachael Ferguson (9)
Stonehouse Primary School, Stonehouse

Mummy

M y mum is the best
U pstairs she plays with me
M y mum's very funny
M y mum's marvellous
Y ellow is her favourite colour.

Ross Cameron (5)
Stonehouse Primary School, Stonehouse

Young Writers Information

We hope you have enjoyed reading this book -
and that you will continue to enjoy it in the coming years.
If you like reading and writing poetry drop us a line, or give us a call,
and we'll send you a free information pack.
Alternatively if you would like to order further copies of this
book or any of our other titles, then please give us a call or log
onto our website at **www.youngwriters.co.uk**

Young Writers Information
Remus House
Coltsfoot Drive
Peterborough
PE2 9JX
(01733) 890066